Hiking the Hooch

A hiker's guide to the trails
of the Chattahoochee River
National Recreation Area

By

Steve Hudson

Hiking the Hooch

A hiker's guide to the trails of the Chattahoochee River National Recreation Area.

By Steve Hudson

Published by

Chattahoochee Media Group
121 Wills Lane
Alpharetta, GA 30009
770 329 7642

www.chattahoocheemedia.com
On Facebook at **www.facebook.com/chattahoocheemedia**

ISBN 978-0-9912606-2-1

Manufactured in the United States

Hiking, like other outdoor activities, is inherently risky. While the information presented here is believed to reflect conditions at the time of publication, neither the author nor the publisher assume any responsibility for the completeness or accuracy of the info presented here, nor for any damages that might be incurred while pursuing any of the activities or visiting any of the locations or hiking in any of the areas described within this book. The user of this book assumes total and complete responsibility for his or her own safety and well-being while on any of the trails described here.

For George Hall,
a great hiking companion
for a lot of years.

Contents

Clockwise from left:
Walkers, joggers and bicyclists enjoy the fitness trail at Cochran Shoals, one of CRNRA's most popular trails; two hikers explore the multifaceted north-end trails of East Palisades; a solitary hiker looks for wildlife along the Johnson Ferry North trail.

Welcome to CRNRA!

Atlanta's Chattahoochee River National Recreation Area is a hiker's dream come true. Here's how to get the most out of exploring it on your own.

August 15, 1978, promised to be a pleasant day in Atlanta. Highs were in the upper 80s...no rain in sight. It would have been a great day for hiking.

The forecast was similar for Washington, DC, where a small crowd gathered in the White House Rose Garden around 9:30 a.m. They were there to see President Jimmy Carter sign H.R. 8336 – legislation which authorized the acquisition of land along a 48-mile section of the Chattahoochee River to create what would become the Chattahoochee River National Recreation Area (CRNRA).

"The President of the United States has many pleasant duties to perform," the President said that morning. "But I don't know of any legislation that I have signed since I've been in the White House, nor will sign while I'm here, that brings me more personal pleasure than does this."

Actually, interest in protecting the river corridor had been simmering since 1971, when there was talk of building a sewer line along the Chattahoochee River. The plan was to literally blast the line's route out of the rocky riverside cliffs in the Palisades area near Interstate 285, Atlanta's perimeter highway. But one group of Atlantans found that plan unacceptable. Calling themselves the "river rats," they went to work lobbying not just legislators but also the public. Their efforts were successful, and the sewer project was relocated.

Following that victory, a group called "Friends of the River" was formed and pushed for regulation of development along the river from Buford Dam downriver to Peachtree Creek. Eventually, their efforts resulted in passage of the Metropolitan River Protection Act in 1973 – and they continued to push for what ultimately became the legislation signed by President Carter on that warm August day in 1978.

The legislation signed by President Carter that morning recognized that "the natural, scenic, recreation, historic, and other values" of that 48-mile stretch of the Hooch "are of special national significance." Further, it noted that "such values should be preserved and protected from developments and uses which would substantially impair or destroy them."

That's how the

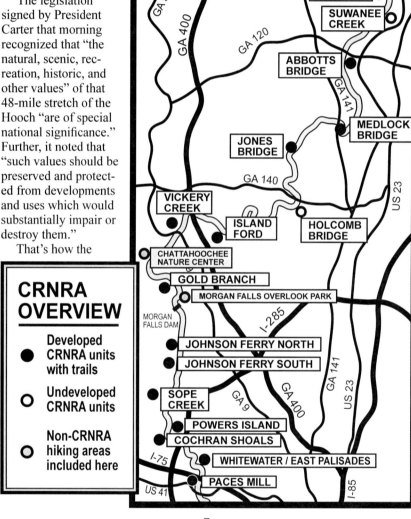

GA 20
Buford Dam
BOWMANS ISLAND
LAUREL RIDGE LOOP
HATCHERY TRAILHEAD
GA 20 / Buford Hwy
ORRS FERRY
Peachtree Industrial Blvd
SETTLES BRIDGE
GA 141
McGINNIS FERRY
GA 9
GA 400
SUWANEE CREEK
GA 120
ABBOTTS BRIDGE
GA 141
MEDLOCK BRIDGE
JONES BRIDGE
US 23
GA 140
VICKERY CREEK
ISLAND FORD
HOLCOMB BRIDGE
CHATTAHOOCHEE NATURE CENTER
GOLD BRANCH
MORGAN FALLS OVERLOOK PARK
MORGAN FALLS DAM
I-285
JOHNSON FERRY NORTH
JOHNSON FERRY SOUTH
GA 141
US 23
SOPE CREEK
GA 9
GA 400
POWERS ISLAND
COCHRAN SHOALS
I-75
WHITEWATER / EAST PALISADES
PACES MILL
US 41
I-85

CRNRA OVERVIEW

● Developed CRNRA units with trails

○ Undeveloped CRNRA units

◎ Non-CRNRA hiking areas included here

7

"Should I take a rain jacket?"

Do you *really* need to carry a rain jacket when hiking CRNRA? There will be times when you won't need it. But there'll be other times when you do...

I recall one hike I made while preparing this book. It was a summer hike, and the projected temperature was in the high 80s with a "typical slight chance of scattered showers." It promised to be a nice day, and I figured that the last thing I needed to worry about was rain.

But partway through my hike a sudden summer shower blew up. It was *cold* rain – and the wind started blowing too. I was drenched within a minute, and since I had *not* brought along my rain jacket I had no way to ward off the deluge as the rain poured down and the wind blew harder and the temperature began to drop. I double-timed it to the car.

By the time I got there I was sure-enough cold – but not so cold that I forgot to make a mental note to *always* put a lightweight rain jacket in the daypack.

Chattahoochee River National Recreation Area (often known simply as "CRNRA") came to be.

Today, CRNRA is administered by the National Park Service and includes a number of developed parcels, or "units," which offer a wide range of recreational opportunities. There are also several as-yet-undeveloped units. These units offer incredible opportunities for outdoor recreation – in particular, miles upon miles of great hiking trails.

"When I moved here from Colorado, I had no idea I'd find this kind of hiking so close to Atlanta," remarked Matt Westborn, a seasoned hiker who has explored trails from coast to coast. Now he hikes in CRNRA almost every week.

"These trails are a treasure," he says. "Atlantans are so lucky to have them."

Indeed, CRNRA's trails offer an incredible array of hiking experiences ranging from flat, gravel-paved pathways ideal for joggers, walkers or parents pushing strollers to heart-pounding climbs and leg-stretching descents. There are trails across wetlands, through bottomlands, and along high ridges. Natural history abounds – wildflowers in spring, brilliant leaves in the fall, wildlife and birds all year long. You'll find human history too in the form of ruins of cabins, forgotten wagon roads, old cemeteries and even ancient rock shelters used by the area's earliest inhabitants. And there are surprises, including musical bamboo and part of what may have been an old still.

Of course, there's also the river. A recreational resource of incalculable value, it's the centerpiece of CRNRA and the thing that ties it all together. It's shaped not only the land itself but also the lives of the people around it, as you'll see when you begin to explore it on your own.

The Chattahoochee River National Recreation Area is a unique and priceless resource. In fact, during that signing ceremony in 1978, President Carter noted that it's "one of the most beautiful places in our country."

And one of the very best ways to see it is on foot – by *hiking the 'Hooch!*

Hiking CRNRA

Since CRNRA is exclusively a day-use area, you don't have to worry about tents and cooking gear and all the other details that overnight camping requires.

Many hikers enjoy CRNRA's riverside trails. But such trails may run very close to the water's edge – and when the water's high, some riverside trails may be submerged.

But it's still hiking, and as with any hiking you've got to cover the basics. Here are some things to remember:

- Wear well-fitting hiking shoes that provide good support
- Wear (and layer) clothing appropriate for the weather
- Let someone know where you're going and when you plan to return

What about equipment? Here are some things to carry which can make your hike more enjoyable.

- *Map.* Many CRNRA unit trails have post-mounted trail maps at key intersections. But all do not. Thus, unless you know a trail well, it's a good idea to carry maps of the trails you're planning on hiking
- *Water and snacks.* A bottle of water and a high-energy snack take up little space in your daypack and can make hiking much more pleasant.
- *Light.* Sometimes hikers lose track of time and end up doing the last leg of a hike at dusk or even in the dark. If that's ever happened to you, then you know how important a light source can be. A small flashlight or LED light doesn't weigh much and takes up little space in your day pack.

- *Camera.* By all means, carry a camera! There are many, many opportunities for fascinating photos along CRNRA's trails.
- *Cell phone.* Carry it just in case. You should have service throughout most or all of the park units.

Snakes (yes, even copperheads) are occasionally seen along these trails. This sign, which makes the point, was spotted trailside at Paces Mill. If you see a snake along a trail, give it room and leave it alone.

What about your *GPS and compass*? Most CRNRA trails are well marked and clearly identified. Even so, it can be fun to carry a GPS or compass to practice your navigation skills – and if by some chance you should become disoriented, those tools can help you figure out where you are.

Finally, leave a *flight plan* letting someone know where you're going. Experienced hikers do that as a matter of course, and you should too.

Hazards along the trail

Hiking in CRNRA, like hiking anywhere, is an outdoor activity that brings with it certain risks. Risks include (among other things) the proximity of the river, unstable or uneven trails, the presence of trailside drop-offs, and natural hazards such as insects and snakes.

As many have noted, one of the joys of CRNRA is that it's a refuge of wilderness in the midst of urbania. But even though much of CRNRA is surrounded by city, it is still a national park and not a developed theme park. The same natural environments that are so enjoyable to explore also pose challenges and risks. Remember that you are solely and completely responsible for your own safety.

What about the river?

As you might expect, the river itself is a ubiquitous presence in CRNRA. You're seldom far from it on these trails. At times its influence can literally be seen (in the thick layers of fog that form on the water) or felt (in the noticeable drop in temperature as you hike trails close to the river).

But sometimes it impacts hiking more directly. The level of the river through CRNRA is primarily determined by what's going on at Buford Dam and at Morgan Falls Dam. When those dams are releasing water, the river will come up. Certain CRNRA trails are only a foot or two from the river's edge, and occasionally those riverside trails may be flooded and impassable.

What if you find part of a trail flooded by high water? Do *not* try to pick your way through the flooded section! That is dangerous and should be strictly avoided, no matter how much you might want to explore beyond the flooded stretch. Instead, save that outing for another day when the river is not so high.

The terrain itself

In CRNRA, as in any outdoor setting, remember that trails can be steep or rough, rocks can be loose or slippery, and your footing can be unstable.

Also be aware of the presence of edges and dropoffs. Some CRNRA trails traverse steep or rocky terrain, and there are places where an edge or dropoff may be very close to the path you're hiking. Within CRNRA, such dropoffs may not be fenced or roped off or otherwise marked. When hiking here, as anywhere, always use extreme caution wherever dropoffs or ledges are present.

Snakes

Snakes, including copperheads, are among the critters you'll occasionally see along these trails. If you see any snake, leave it alone. Don't poke it with a stick or move in for "one more photo." Just don't!

Stinging insects

A more likely critter-type hazard is a nest of yellow jackets or wasps. Yellow jackets nest among rocks, in hollow logs, and in similar places. Hornets can build nests that hang from low branches. Wasps build nests under sheltering overhangs (including bridge handrails and trailside maps). Twice this past year I found active wasp nests under the post-mounted maps at various trail intersections. For anyone, stings hurt! For those with allergies, however, a sting can be life-threatening. If you're allergic, always carry the appropriate emergency medications and know how to use them to deal with a sting.

What about ticks?

Ticks are another buggy hazard. The best way to deal with 'em is to avoid 'em. Use a repellent, tuck pants into your socks, check yourself after your hike, and remove any attached ticks promptly and correctly.

Here's how the CDC advises removal of ticks. You'll find more info at http://www.cdc.gov/ticks/removing_a_tick.html.

1) Use fine-tipped tweezers to grasp the tick as close to the skin as you can.

2) Gently pull upward with steady, even pressure. Do not twist or jerk, as that can cause the mouth-parts to break off, leaving them in the skin.

3) After removal, disinfect the area as well as your hands with rubbing alcohol, an iodine scrub, or soap and water. Over the next few weeks, if you develop a rash at the bite site (particularly in a bulls-eye pattern, which could be a sign of Lyme disease) or develop a fever, check with your doctor.

CDC advises avoiding folk remedies such as painting the tick with nail polish or using heat to make it let go. As CDC notes, the goal is to remove the tick as quickly as possible, not to wait for it to let go on its own.

Poison ivy

Finally, remember that poison ivy loves to grow along trails in the south. Learn what it looks like and avoid it as much as possible. If you come in contact with it, wash the area well with soap and water when you return home.

How to use this guide

Hiking the Hooch is designed to help you enjoy the great trails of CRNRA. Starting at the Bowmans Island Unit on CRNRA's north end, this guide works its way south with a detailed look at the hiking opportunities in each developed CRNRA unit along the way. Units which are currently undeveloped are not covered since they include no officially developed trails.

Each section includes detailed trail maps which are keyed to the accompanying trail description. Some maps also include National Park Service intersection identifiers; on those maps, these NPS identifiers are boxed. For example, $\boxed{\text{SC3}}$ marks the intersection which the Park Service identifies as point SC3.

In keeping with the spirit of this guide, several closely related but non-CRNRA hikes are also covered here. These include the Laurel Ridge Trail, a Corps of Engineers trail accessible from the Bowmans Island Unit's northern trailhead; the boardwalk wetlands loop at the Chattahoochee Nature Center; and the Morgan Falls Overlook Trail, a City of Sandy Springs trail near Morgan Falls Dam.

So pack your day pack and snug up those hiking shoes. It's time to start *hiking the Hooch!*

If you've done much hiking, you know that most trail systems are dynamic things. Especially in an area such as CRNRA, where trail development is ongoing, it's always possible that an existing trail will be rerouted or closed – or that an altogether new one will be opened. If you encounter such changed conditions, drop us a note and we'll include the info in the next edition of Hiking the Hooch!

The pros agree: one of the best ways to get the most out of hiking the trails of CRNRA is to slow down and savor the experience.

What the rangers say

Thoughts on how to get the most from hiking CRNRA – from some of the people who know it best.

CRNRA has been called "Atlanta's back yard. An impressive backyard it is, too, with river and woods and more than enough outdoors to make you forget you're in the big city.

How can you get the most out of your hiking adventures in the units of CRNRA? I wanted to find out from the experts. So I posed the question to some of the folks at park headquarters, including chief of park operations Scott Pfeninger, and supervisory park ranger Sean Perchalski.

I thought I might get answers of the "see-this-and-don't-miss-that" variety. But I heard something else instead. What I heard is that the way to get the most out of hiking CRNRA is to immerse yourself in it and allow the park to speak to you – or, Scott puts it, to "keep your eyes open, to look and listen and feel."

"Use your sniffer too," Scott adds. From wildflowers in spring to muscadines in the fall to the unique aroma of the woods all year long, your nose can add a whole new dimension to the CRNRA experience.

Scott and Sean both agree that a great way to get a good overview of the area is to float through it on the river. But to experience it more completely, adds Sean, it's hard to beat exploration on foot.

"Hike to the center of one of the units, then stop and look around," he suggests.

Is there a best season to visit?

Spring is always popular, bringing warming weather as the landscape awakens from winter. So is summer, though the heat and humidity keep many hikers at home in the air conditioning.

Fall, with cooler temperatures and changing leaves, is the favorite season for many CRNRA hiking enthusiasts.

"A nice fall weekend can be as busy here as the Fourth of July," Scott says.

And don't overlook winter. Like many experienced hikers, both Sean and Scott are fans of wintertime in the park. The leaves are off the trees, and the views can be spectacular.

Even during peak seasons, it's possible to find solitude if you hike on a weekday – especially during the middle of the day. Give it a try. You just may have the trails completely to yourself.

No matter when you visit, Scott and Sean agree, the key is to slow down and savor the adventure. Yes, running through the parkland on an after-work jog is popular.

"But it's not the best way to *experience* the park," Scott says.

Now what about those don't-miss places? That list of places will be different for every hiker.

"Walking a trail is a very personal experience," says CRNRA facility management specialist Charlie Jackson. Charlie is a fan of history, for example, and he has a special affinity for sites large or small with historical significance. There are many such places within CRNRA, and he enjoys imagining what they might have been like in years past.

He's also fond of places where there's no visible sign of being in the big city, no matter which way you look.

"There are places in the park where you won't see anything to remind you that you're in the city," he says. "When I find a place like that, it really moves me."

Places such as those (Scott described them as places where you can "listen to the solitude") truly are treasures, and there are plenty

Staying safe in CRNRA

CRNRA gets about 3.5 million visitors each year, and the vast majority are good folks. In fact, according to supervisory park ranger Sean Perchalski, the biggest problem he encounters is people who don't keep their dogs on leash (or who don't clean up behind their dogs)!

But with all those visitors, there's going to be a bad apple once in a while – and that brings up the subject of crime in the park.

For the most part, CRNRA is a very safe place to enjoy the outdoors.

"The recreation area is safe," says Sean, "and crimes against persons are almost nonexistent."

But a problem that does occur now and then is that of car break-ins.

"Car break-ins are almost always crimes of opportunity," he says, adding that they're usually triggered by items left in plain view in a car.

"Don't leave valuables in plain sight in your vehicle," he says. "Put them in your trunk or under your seat *before* you arrive."

Overall, Scott says, CRNRA is a very safe park.

"Criminals don't go to the woods," he says.

of them awaiting you on the trails of CRNRA – starting with the trails of the Bowmans Island Unit, which we'll look at in the next chapter.

A hiker arrives at the northern trailhead for the Bowmans Island Unit trails. This trailhead is accessed via the first Corps of Engineers' Lower Pool Park parking area near Buford Dam.

Bowmans Island Unit

This northernmost CRNRA unit boasts riverside hiking and upland trails – plus easy access to Buford Dam and to a major trout rearing station too.

The northernmost unit of the Chattahoochee River National Recreation Area is the Bowmans Island Unit. It begins just downriver from Buford Dam (which forms Lake Lanier) and extends to the Georgia Department of Natural Resources' trout rearing station more than two miles to the south. Within the unit are trails which can be mixed and matched to create a number of great hikes.

There are two trailheads. The northern one is reached via the Army Corps of

Finding the trailheads

Southern trailhead from GA 400: Exit at GA 20 (exit 14) and go east for about 4.5 miles to River Club Drive (it's the entrance to a residential area). There's a Department of Natural Resources sign at the turn. Turn left on River Club Drive. Go about a half mile to Trout Place Road and turn right. The road ends at the Georgia DNR trout rearing facility. Hiker parking is in the indicated area along the side of the road *before* the gate. When parking, be aware that the shoulder drops off fairly steeply in some places.

Northern trailhead (via Lower Pool Park at Buford Dam) from GA 400: Exit at GA 20 (exit 14) and go east for about 0.3 miles to Market Place Blvd. Turn left and go 0.8 miles to Buford Dam Road. Turn right and go roughly 4.3 miles to Lower Pool West Road on your right. Turn right and go down the hill toward the river. Park in the first parking area on your right. The well-marked trailhead is at a corner of the parking area.

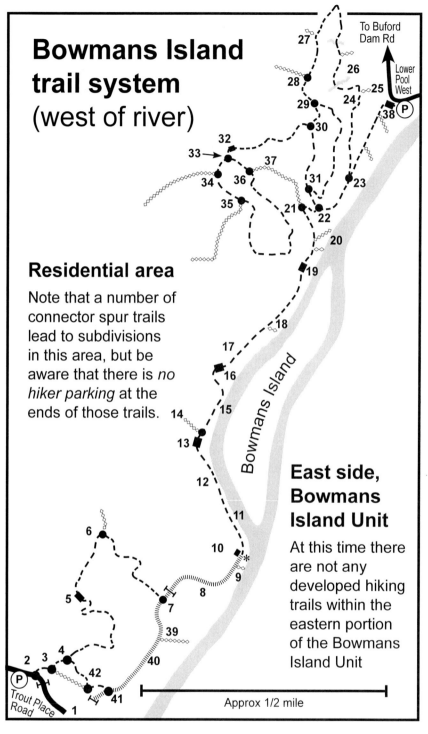

Bowmans Island trail system (west of river)

To Buford Dam Rd

Lower Pool West

Residential area

Note that a number of connector spur trails lead to subdivisions in this area, but be aware that there is *no hiker parking* at the ends of those trails.

Bowmans Island

East side, Bowmans Island Unit

At this time there are not any developed hiking trails within the eastern portion of the Bowmans Island Unit

Trout Place Road

Approx 1/2 mile

Engineers' Lower Pool Park near Buford Dam, while the southern one is near the Georgia Department of Natural Resources' trout rearing station at the end of Trout Place Road.

Be sure you understand the parking situation at these trailheads. On the south end, hiker parking is along the road *outside* the gate to the trout rearing facility. It has definite closing hours, and when it closes the gate is closed too. You don't want to return from a hike after closing time only to find your car on the wrong side of a closed gate.

Similarly, note the posted closing times for the northern parking area near Buford Dam. The gate on the road from Buford Dam Road to the parking areas is closed at the posted time; again, you do not want your car to be inside the gate when the road is closed at the end of the day.

As you hike here, you'll note several connector trails linking the trail system to nearby residential areas. However, there is *no hiker parking* at the end of those connectors. Thus, hikers should park in the designated trailhead parking areas.

The south loop

The first hike we'll cover is the south-end loop hike. By all means visit the **trout rearing station (1)** near the trailhead; it provides trout for stocking into several Georgia streams and rivers (including the nearby Chattahoochee). This is a favorite destination among kids, and there's even an organized tour every Saturday at 1 p.m. During that tour you'll learn about the fish and about how the facility works – and maybe you'll get to feed the trout too!

The CRNRA trailhead is outside the trout rearing facility gate, behind several large rocks and a large sign with a fish on it. Be sure that you follow the hiking trail and not the private driveway immediately to the left of the trailhead.

The trail curves right as it climbs, and you'll soon spot an **intersection (3)** with a rough spur trail which turns right and follows the DNR facility's fence-line. Fishermen sometimes use that spur as a shortcut to the river. Just beyond the spur is a cluster of informational signs. Stay on the main trail.

The main trail soon brings you to an **intersection (4)** with a trail that goes left and up the hill – the beginning of the southern loop. We'll hike this loop clockwise, so turn left at point 4. The trail climbs for a bit, then drops through switchbacks to a **bridge (5)** over a creek.

Beyond the bridge, the trail continues to **intersection 6,** the first of several intersections with connector trails which leave CRNRA and lead to nearby residential areas. There is no hiker parking available at the end of the connector, so turn right to continue the loop on the main trail.

The trail continues through the forest and soon begins a descent to **intersection 7** with a wide, level graveled road. To your left, this road extends upriver to a **warning siren (10)** which alerts river users to the start of water release from Buford Dam. To your right it goes back toward the trout facility.

Turn right to continue the south loop. You'll soon see a **spur (39)** leading toward the river – one of many to-the-river spurs along the riverside portion of the Bowmans Island trails. Not far beyond that spur the road will **ford a creek (40)**.

The trail soon bends right and comes to **intersection 41,** where a dirt trail goes right and up the hill while the gravel road continues a few dozen yards before ending at a service gate. Turn right on that dirt trail to continue the loop. You'll climb to **intersection 42,** the other end of that fisherman's spur,

The "fish sign trailhead" near the entrance to the Georgia Department of Natural Resources trout rearing station at the southern end of the Bowmans Island trail system.

but stay on the main trail up the hill. Notice the rocks outcropping on the hillside to your right as approach **intersection 4** and the end of the loop. From there, it's just a short distance back to the trailhead at point 2.

Central connector

What if you turned left at **intersection 7** and continued upriver instead of heading back toward the trout rearing facility? That puts you on the connector linking the southern loop with the northern loop trails near Buford Dam. You'll pass through a gate just beyond the intersection; the road then curves right, crosses a **clearing (8)** and passes another **spur (9)** that heads toward the river.

Beyond the spur you'll soon arrive at one of several **warning sirens (10)** which alert river users to the start of water release from Buford Dam. A small block building sits on one side of the trail, while the siren itself is on a pole on the other side.

The gravel road ends at the siren, but a footpath continues into the woods beyond. At first the trail follows a tunnel through the undergrowth, but that soon gives way to more open riverside forest. Unexpectedly, a **metal bench swing (11)** appears on your right at a vantage point roughly even with the downstream end of Bowmans Island.

The trail continues, splitting and rejoining at a rocky area and then crossing a **bridge (13)** over a creek. Beyond the bridge another **spur (14)** goes left toward

One of the many foot bridges on the central connector trail linking the northern and southern parts of the Bowmans Island trail network.

a residential area – but stay on the main trail. You'll soon cross a wide, shallow **gully (15),** then another **bridge (16)** followed by a **ford (17)** over a wet-weather branch. Soon, another **spur (18)** heads to the right toward the river. This strip of CRNRA is narrow, so you may see houses through the trees off to your left.

You're now nearing the upper end of Bowman's Island. Another **bridge (19)** carries you over a rocky stream, which can be very scenic after a rain. Beyond it several **spur trails (20)** go right and crisscross the floodplain between trail and river. Ferns are thick not only on the floodplain but also on the nearby hillside.

Swinging left, the trail turns away from the river and follows a creek upstream. You'll hear this creek splashing over rocks before you see it. Then, almost before you know it, you're at **intersection 21**– the end

Among the things you'll see on the central connector are this small block house and the accompanying warning siren (on the pole near the center of photo). The siren warns of water releases from Buford Dam. The warning sign at right spells out the danger of fast-rising water following a release.

18

of the central connector trail and the beginning of the northern cluster of trails.

The northern trails

The northern suite of trails at Bowmans Island consists of two loops (which we'll call the "big loop" and the "little loop") with a short connector trail between them... plus several interior trails. And if you go just north of the CRNRA unit, there's also an easy stroll to a great view of the spillway at Buford Dam.

Easiest access to these trails is from the northern trailhead at the first Corps of Engineers parking area on Lower Pool West Road (which turns south from Buford Dam Road). You can also explore these trails as part of a much more ambitious hike starting at the southern trailhead (near the fish rearing facility). But this guide will start at the trailhead at the unit's north end.

The CRNRA trailhead is at the back of the parking area near info signs. Beyond the signs, the trail immediately crosses a **bridge (38)** over a creek. Pick your way through the horse barrier at the end of the bridge and then go left, following a mostly-straight trail that's heavily used by fishermen. You'll pass several spur trails leading left; fishermen use those too.

You'll soon reach **intersection 23** with the "big loop." Turn right and head uphill. Cross an overgrown clearing on an occasionally rough section of trail (watch your footing); then re-enter woods and begin a long climb. The trail reaches a high point after about 200 yards; there, look left for some clusters of stones that suggest the presence of an old house site. Just beyond them, a short spur trail leads to a rocky point that provides a **view of the river (25)** far below, especially when the leaves are off the trees.

Continue on across a **small branch (26).** Just beyond it a spur trail goes right, and you'll cross a tiny wet-weather branch about 150 feet beyond the spur.

The trail, at this point heading north, is about to make a sharp bend to the left. Houses can be seen through the trees to your right.

Soon after the bend a steep **spur (27)** goes right. Then, about 40 yards beyond that point, a **very prominent spur (28)** turns right between two wood posts at a large "PEDESTRIAN TRAIL" sign. It's one of several connector trails which lead out of CRNRA and into neighboring subdivisions. There's no hiker parking at the end of those connectors, however, so unless you live in one of the subdivisions you should stay on the main trail toward **intersection 29**.

At that intersection you can go right or left. Going left puts you on a wide, sometimes rutted trail that follows a ridge before descending to rejoin the "big loop" at point 31. To explore the "little loop," however, go right to **intersection 30** and then turn more or less west along a connector trail. You'll cross a **bridge (32)** over a creek; just beyond it is **intersection 33** with the "little loop."

Go right at 33 to hike counterclockwise around the little loop. You'll soon come to **intersection 34** (another of those subdivision connector spurs) and then **intersection 35** (yet another subdivision spur). At each of those intersections, stay left to remain on the little loop. Again, there's no hiker parking at the end of either of those spurs.

Beyond point 35 the loop swings south, then east, and then turns back to the north and northwest as it climbs toward **point 36.** This intersection with a faint spur is very hard to spot, although the spur is worth exploring...but it's much more easily explored from the other end (via **intersection 21).** Thus, stay on the obvious main trail, continuing a winding path toward point 33.

At 33, turn right and backtrack along the connector to point 30. Then turn right (south, toward point 31) to explore the remaining portion of the big loop. Stay on the main trail through 31, following a rocky and curving descent downhill to **intersection 22.** That's an important intersection to Bowmans Island hikers, since turning right at that point puts you on the connector leading south toward the southern trails and the fish rearing facility.

To complete the northern trails hike, go straight ahead at 22 to stay on the main trail. It curves left as it makes a short descent back to the river floodplain and **intersection 23** – and then on to the parking area where you began.

The 21-to-36 spur

One nice diversion in the Bowmans Island Unit is the spur trail linking point 21 on the main connector with point 36 on the little loop. It can be accessed from either end, but access from **intersection 21** is by far the easiest.

Start at **intersection 21** on the north-south connector. Instead of making the ford and hiking toward point 22, follow the spur that goes up the creek. It leads

Is this rusting relic (found in a small creek along the 21-to-36 spur) part of an old still? Some say it is.

you to a ford (at a sometimes slightly wobbly rock) and then fords the creek a second time near a **sandy area (37).** Once there, look for a large and rusting iron object sitting partly buried in the creek.

"I think it's part of an old still," one hiker surmised. "Those old-time moonshiners liked a good water source, and this little creek would have been perfect."

Also look to the left for an interesting little rock outcrop partway up the hill.

Beyond this point the trail fades as it makes a steep scramble up to intersection 36 and the big loop. Alternately, backtrack to intersection 21 and continue your adventure from there.

The spillway overlook

Although it's not part of CRNRA, the footbridge overlooking the Buford

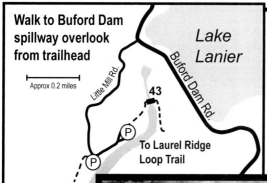

Walk to Buford Dam spillway overlook from trailhead

Approx 0.2 miles

Little Mill Rd.

Buford Dam Rd.

Lake Lanier

43

P

P

To Laurel Ridge Loop Trail

The pedestrian bridge over the Buford Dam spillway is easily accessible from the Bowmans Island northern trailhead and makes a great sidetrip – especially if you can time it to catch a release from Buford Dam.

Dam spillway is an easy stroll from the northern Bowmans Island trailhead and is something that many hikers detour to see. From the trailhead park-

ing area, hike through and beyond the second parking area toward Buford Dam. Cross a **large grassy field (43)** and head toward the dam, approaching as you do so a **pedestrian bridge (44)** over the Buford Dam spillway. All water released from Buford Dam flows through that spillway, and when a water release begins it's something of a minor attraction. From the bridge, you can watch the water rise as power generation or water releases begin, and it's impressive to see how quickly the river level comes up once the water begins to flow. Find out water release times by calling (770) 945-1466.

Beyond the end of the bridge is a connector which takes you to the Corps of Engineers Laurel Ridge Loop Trail (described on the next two pages). Although not part of CRNRA, it's a neat trail that fits well in this guide.

The east side of the river?

When you hike these trails, you'll be on the west side of the river. But there's a lot of CRNRA land on the east side too. What about hiking there?

At this time, there are no developed trails in the eastern portion of the Bowmans Island Unit. However, the Corps of Engineers' Laurel Ridge Loop Trail provides some great hiking on the east side. It also provides access to a short spur trail which extends into the Bowmans Island Unit and provides a tantalizing glimpse of the hiking possibilities that this area may someday offer.

By the way, much CRNRA trail construction is done by volunteers. But in units farther from Atlanta volunteers are harder to come by. Consider becoming a CRNRA volunteer and doing your part to help make those new trails a reality.

The Laurel Ridge Loop Trail

A s of this writing there are no developed trails in the eastern part of the Bowmans Island Unit. However, a very good Corps of Engineers trail – the Laurel Ridge Loop – is nearby. It offers almost four miles of good hiking and also connects with a spur leading into the eastern part of the Bowmans Island Unit – perhaps offering a preview of what's to come.

Even though the loop is not a CRNRA trail, it fits well with the intent of this guide and so is included here.

There are many access points for this trail; we'll start at the CRNRA Bowmans Island trailhead in the first parking area on the west side of the river. Walk up the road through the second parking area and across a **field (1)** to the **bridge (2)** over the Buford Dam spillway. Across the bridge, follow the trail to the right, eventually crossing a **long fishing bridge (3)** and then climbing to **intersection 4** with the loop. Turn right.

A Laurel Ridge Loop hiker takes on that steep set of steps at point 18 near the dam.

The trail follows the river for about a quarter mile, then swings left and passes **two spurs (5)** which mark undeveloped trails leading into CRNRA's Bowmans Island Unit. Beyond the spurs, you'll traverse several bridges and boardwalks before **crossing a road (6)**. Beyond that road crossing another bridge awaits, followed by a power line clearing and (after re-entering the woods) the rusted **remains of an old, old car (7)**.

After another **road crossing (8)**, the trail turns right at a playground and follows a **paved walkway (9)** around a parking area to **intersection 10**.

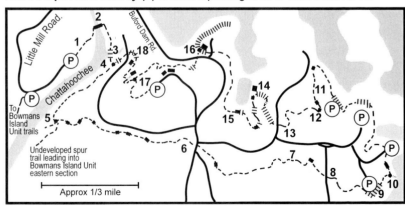

There, a spur leads to a lakeside platform. The main trail goes left, crossing a long bridge. It soon traverses another parking area, then re-enters the woods and (at a large field) follows more paved walkway around another parking area. You'll eventually re-enter woods, albeit briefly, and then climb some concrete steps before skirting yet another parking area on a paved walkway.

The trail continues beyond the lot, crossing a bridge and then traversing a set of **timber steps (11)** and a pair of boardwalks. Beyond them you'll cross a **narrow clearing (12)**. The trail widens somewhat, then trends right and passes through a stretch **lined with large stones (13).** Some massive boulders will be visible to the right, and then you cross another road.

Beyond the road is an extensive wetlands area, which you cross mostly

Among the surprises along the Laurel Ridge Loop are the rusting remains of an old car.

on boardwalks. It's prime birding territory – and prime mosquito habitat too. Keep swatting, and you'll get through it.

The path soon comes to a **pond and cabin (14)** where it turns left. More wetlands (and mosquitoes) follow. You'll soon cross a **clearing (15)** and another road. Beyond that road, follow a sidewalk around the back of a restroom building and turn left at an **intersection (16)** near the first picnic table.

The trail continues to another road crossing; beyond it, stone steps climb back into the woods. You'll cross a tiny boardwalk and then pass behind a cluster of buildings before arriving at **intersection 17**. A left at that point takes you on a looping path alongside a parking area; go right to continue the loop. You'll notice a spur leading back to a deck, but stay on the main trail.

Soon, you'll come to an observation deck located on the left side of the trail. Beyond it you'll descend a set of extremely steep stone steps, followed by equally steep set of wood steps, followed by a short boardwalk – and then a road crossing. From there, it's just a short distance to **intersection 4** and the end of the Laurel Ridge Loop Trail.

This bridge carries Laurel Ridge Loop hikers across an arm of Lake Lanier

Settles Bridge

There's only a little hiking at Settles Bridge, but that's no problem because the bridge is the thing.

The iron and steel structure known as Settles Bridge, the centerpiece of the Settles Bridge Unit, was built in the late 1890s to replace a ferry which had been operated there by the Settles family. It was used into the 1950s, but all that remains now is massive support columns and a river-spanning iron frame that floats over the water as if suspended by mist and fog. It's all oddly enchanting.

This is a relatively undeveloped unit of CRNRA, and there's currently not a lot to be found there in the way of hiking. A short gravel trail leads from the parking area to the old bridge, and short trails lead from the vicinity of the bridge up and down the river. But it's still a neat area that's definitely worth checking out.

A **cleared right-of-way (1)** (which may be overgrown) extends from each end of the parking area. The trailhead is near the back center of the parking area to the left of a cluster of signs. A wide and

Finding the trailhead

From GA 400: Take Georgia 20 east. Cross the Chattahoochee and look for Suwanee Dam Road. Turn right. Go 1.4 miles to Johnson Road and turn right. Go 1.1 miles to Settles Bridge Road (you'll pass Settles Bridge Park, a Gwinnett County park, on your right along the way) and turn right. Initially paved, Settles Bridge Road quickly becomes gravel. Follow it for about 0.9 miles to the Settles Bridge Unit parking area.

curving **graveled path (2)** leads into the woods toward the river. To its left you'll immediately see signs of the bridge there among the trees – rusting iron support structures now supporting nothing but memories.

The path ends at a long, two-stage **pedestrian ramp (3)** that provides easy access to a **raft and canoe launch (4).** Spur trails cut around the ramp to the left and right. The **bridge (5)** itself is just a few yards downriver.

From the ramp, you'll notice well-used fisherman's trails going upriver and downriver. Look at the downstream trail first. It begins at an **intersection (6)** near the ramp, soon passing what appears to be an **old wagon road (7)** that goes left but quickly becomes overgrown. Beyond that point the trail continues for a short distance before turning right and ending at a **sharp drop to the river (8).**

What about upstream? Another well-used trail heads upstream from

Traces of the old bridge seem to be growing among the trees.

intersection 9 near the ramp. It soon crosses a deep and steep-sided **gully (10).** Beyond the gully the trail soon enters a clearing; there, a **spur trail (11)** turns right and soon intersects the long right-of-way clearing extending from the parking area. If the clearing is not overgrown, you can turn right and walk along the clearing to return to the parking area.

Trails of Settles Bridge

12

10
9
11
4
5
3 2
6
1
P
7
Right-of-way clearing
Settles Bridge Rd
1
Approx. 0.1 mile
8

If you stay on the main trail beyond the spur, you'll soon come to a deep **creek channel (12)** where the trail turns right and follows the creek upstream. CRNRA maps show park land continuing across the creek and up the river for quite a ways. But at this time most CRNRA hikers stop at that creek (especially if the river is high and has backed up water into the creek channel) and then backtrack to the parking area.

25

Abbotts Bridge

The coolest thing about Abbotts Bridge (if you believe Jennie Sue) just may be the enchanted trees.

Tucked between the river, a major road, an office development, and a soccer field complex, the Abbotts Bridge Unit doesn't have a lot of room for hiking trails. But what it lacks in quantity it makes up in whimsy.

Just ask six-year-old Jennie Sue. She'll explain it all.

I met Jennie Sue and her mom one Saturday not too long ago. I was out for a quick stroll, and the short and easy Abbotts Bridge Trail was perfect. I was heading for the trail just as Jennie Sue and her mom were finishing a hike of their own. We met near the trailhead.

"Hey Mister!" she said. "Are you gonna go see the *trees?*"

"Jennie Sue," said her mom, "you can't just talk to –"

"Oh-Mama-I-know," Jennie Sue said. "But he needs to know about the *trees*. And *you know why!*" Jennie Sue paused, then added, "Should we *tell* him?"

Silence hung in the air for a second. Then –

"Trees?" I said.

"YES!" said Jennie Sue. "That's what I'm *trying* to *tell you!* Tell him, Mama! Tell him about the *trees!*"

"Well..." her mom began.

"They're ENCHANTED!" proclaimed Jennie Sue. "You'll see!"

Mom looked at daughter and then at me.

"Well," the mom said after a moment, "they do kind of *look* enchanted. If you use your imagination..."

"That's *right!*" said Jennie Sue, who was turning out to be a child of a thou-

26

sand exclamation points. "You'll see!"

"Jennie Sue has a vivid imagination," said the mom as she took Jennie Sue by the hand and tugged the little girl in the direction of the parking lot.

But Jennie Sue was not so easily moved.

"I *do* have imageration!" Jennie Sue said. "I *do!* But they *are* enchanted trees!" To her mom she said, "*You* said the elves and the faeries live in them! They live in the holes in the tree trunks. *You* said you saw them. And *he'll* see them too. Mister, you'll see them if you *look!*"

"Cool!" I offered, not quite knowing what else to say.

I'm sure that Jennie Sue and her mom were going to have one of those "don't talk to strangers" talks later on. But right at that moment – right there at the top of the Abbotts Bridge boat ramp, there was a question hanging in the air. And trees were at the center of it.

There was no doubt about it. I was going to have to go looking for these enchanted trees myself.

I waved goodbye to Jennie Sue and her mom and stepped onto the trail and into the woods.

The Abbotts Bridge Unit riverside trail

CRNRA's Abbotts Bridge Unit is located just off Abbotts Bridge Road. It's not a large unit, and it doesn't have the extensive trail network that you'll find in some other CRNRA units. In fact, this unit tempts hikers with only a single path: a relatively short riverside trail.

Near the boat ramp, the trail gets a fair amount of use and is clear and well-defined. But toward its downstream end it gets less use and may be overgrown and somewhat harder to follow. That may be because this is an in-and-out trail; in other words, you hike it to the end and then backtrack to your starting point. No loop hike is possible without leaving CRNRA land.

Despite those considerations, the trail is ideal for a quick hike. It can be a good birdwatching trail, and it just may be a perfect place for a quick stretching of legs – or for a short hike with your kids.

The unit's entry is on Abbotts Bridge Road just east of the river and just past a sand and gravel business (as you're heading east). The entry is clearly marked by a large sign; turning at the sign puts you on a long gravel access road that leads you to the unit's parking area.

Once at the parking area, you'll see a large covered **pavilion (1)** just south of the parking area and a **restroom building (2)** just to the east. To the west of the parking area is the unit's boat ramp, popular with a variety of river users. Boaters and other floating river users will be interested to know that, as of this writing, the Abbotts Bridge restroom building is the first riverside restroom you'll come to when floating downstream from Buford Dam.

The Abbotts Bridge Unit's hiking trail begins at a trailhead located immediately adjacent to the downstream side of the boat ramp. From the boat ramp, it's

Finding the trailhead:

From I-285: Take exit 31B (Peachtree Industrial Blvd./SR 141 North). Go north 12.4 miles to Abbotts Bridge Road/GA120. Turn left and go 0.6 miles to the unit entrance, which will be on your left just before you cross the river.

From I-85: Take exit 107 (Duluth Highway/SR 120). Go west about 6.4 miles through Duluth to the unit entrance on the left. If you cross the river, you've gone too far.

From GA 400: Take exit 10 (Old Milton Parkway/SR 120) and go east about 7.8 miles to the unit. Be sure to continue straight on Abbotts Bridge Rd. when SR 120 turns left. The unit will be on your right soon after you cross the river.

not immediately clear that the path leading away downstream from the boat ramp is in fact a trail. But it is, and once you're on the trail and make the downriver turn as you reach the river the route will be distinct and clear.

This trail is not a long one by CRNRA standards. In fact, depending on where you decide the trail stops (and that may be a function of the

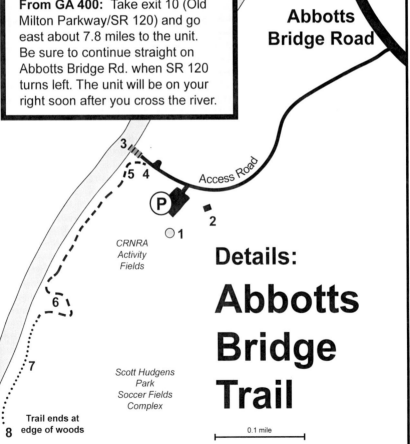

Abbotts Bridge Road

3

5 4

Access Road

P

2

CRNRA Activity Fields

1

6

7

Scott Hudgens Park Soccer Fields Complex

Trail ends at edge of woods

8

Details:

Abbotts Bridge Trail

0.1 mile

seasonal undergrowth that tends to choke the southern portion of the trail) it may not offer even a quarter mile of hiking each way.

Start by looking for the trail head near the **Abbotts Bridge Unit boat ramp (3).** The **trail head (4)** itself is at the top end of the boat ramp on the ramp's downstream side. It goes straight toward the river for a few yards, then turns left and downriver.

And that's when you'll see the first of Jennie Sue's **enchanted trees (5).**

The trees – actually a number of very impressive oaks – definitely have a certain magic about them. They're huge, and their trunks are convoluted and textured with many little nooks and crannies where I'm sure Jennie Sue's elves and faeries would happily stop for break any time they happen to be passing through.

If you're lucky enough to hike the trail following a summer rainshower, you'll find that the colors are even richer and more intense – and when the sunlight finally breaks through and hits the textured bark and rich green leaves, it only enhances the fantasy-like feeling of the scene. Abundant and very healthy

The Abbotts Bridge trail begins at this trailhead just to the left of the boat ramp.

poison ivy notwithstanding, I found myself lingering there and spending much longer than I'd expected I would simply enjoying the spectacle of those trees.

Beyond the trees, the trail continues downriver. Eventually it swings away from the river to **cross a small channel (6).** The channel is often filled with water, particularly when the river's high, but an easy crossing is some distance up the cut and is dry.

At some point along this trail, you may realize that the path you're following is becoming more narrow and less distinct. The reason? The farther you go on this trail, the less it appears to be used. As a result, the **lower section of the trail (7)** may be harder to follow than the upper portion nearer the boat ramp. For that reason, most hikers turn back at some point. But if you continue to the very end, you'll find that the trail ends at the **edge of the woods (8)** where the woods meet the soccer fields.

If you make it that far, turn around and backtrack the way you came in to stay on CRNRA land.

Medlock Bridge

This unit offers not only intriguing trails and great riverside scenery but some challenging hiking too.

The Medlock Bridge Unit, like many other CRNRA units, is named for the bridge that crossed the river here in years gone by. The unit is located directly off Medlock Bridge Road/Peachtree Parkway/SR-141. That makes access quick and easy. Note, however, that it's a very heavily traveled highway. Simply turning into or out of the unit can be an experience – particularly during rush hour, which in this part of the city seems to be most of the day.

Once you make that turn, however, the world suddenly simplifies. Indeed, the Medlock Bridge Unit is a perfect antidote to urban stress. You'll often meet after-work hikers who have chosen to spend rush hour enjoying this unit's trails instead of sitting "out there" in a traffic jam with 10,000 other commuters.

"The traffic's terrible right now," one of them told me the other day, "so instead of fighting it I decided to go hiking for a while till the madness on the roads dies down."

If you ask me, that's a pretty good call.

This unit's trails conveniently break down into three separate hikes: a short loop located between the parking area and Peachtree Parkway; the riverside trail, a surprisingly challeng-

Finding the trailhead:

From Georgia 400: Take exit 10 (Old Milton Parkway/SR-120) and go east for 6.2 miles to SR-141 (Medlock Bridge Road). Turn right and go about 4 miles. You'll cross the river, and the entrance to the Medlock Bridge Unit will be on your left. Use caution when making the turn into the unit, as traffic is usually heavy – and *fast*.

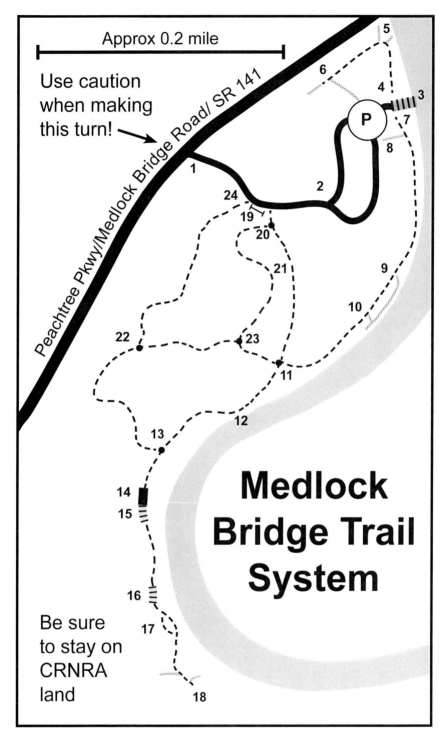

Approx 0.2 mile

Use caution
when making
this turn!

Peachtree Pkwy/Medlock Bridge Road/ SR 141

P

**Medlock
Bridge Trail
System**

Be sure
to stay on
CRNRA
land

ing in-and-out hike along the river; and an interior hike which includes not only river floodplain hiking but also some hiking up (and down) and along ridges.

All hikes begin at the parking area off Peachtree Parkway/SR141. The **main entry (1)** is clearly marked, but the turn into the entry can be tricky. There is lots of traffic on Peachtree Parkway, so use extreme caution making the turn. Use even more caution as you exit back onto Peachtree Parkway.

Once in the park, follow the access road to the parking area. You'll pass a **gate (19)**, one of the access points to the interior trails. Continue past the gate to a **fork in the road (2)** where you must go right to reach the parking area.

The short loop

If you've only got a little while to hike, you'll enjoy the short loop north of the parking area. It begins just to the left of the unit's **boat ramp (3)**. Facing the river from the top of the ramp, the short loop **trail head (4)** will be on your left.

The trail heads downriver, turning left as you near Peachtree Parkway. **Two faint and very short spur trails (5)** go off to the right at the bend in the trail, but stay on the main trail which is now running essentially parallel to Peachtree Parkway. You'll hear (and probably see) traffic off to your right.

The trail becomes obviously less heavily used as you follow it through this stretch. Many hikers simply backtrack at some point and return to the boat ramp the way they came, but others look for an **intersection with a short connector (6)** which leads back to the parking lot. The parking lot end of that connector exits the woods next to a blue "Shuttle Bus Stop" sign; from there, cross the parking lot to return to the boat ramp where you began.

The riverside trail

The Medlock Bridge Unit's riverside trail follows the river upstream for more than a half mile, offering everything from essentially level riverside hiking to steep, muscle-stretching climbs and descents. It's a particularly scenic riverside hike, too, and veteran CRNRA hikers generally recommend it highly.

The trailhead for this hike is at the top of the **boat ramp (3)**. As you're facing the river, look for the **trailhead (7)** on your right. Follow the trail upstream.

About 50 paces down the trail, a connector trail turns right and leads to an area with several **picnic tables (8)**, then continues on to the parking area. You'll also find other picnic tables tucked away in the woods around the parking area.

The main trail continues upriver. After about 250 yards look for an **intersection (9)** with a spur trail going off to the left and down toward the river. That spur runs very close to the river and parallels the main trail for about 75 paces, at which point a **very short connector (10)** links it back to the main trail. Beyond that connector, the spur deteriorates quickly and should be avoided. The main trail, however, continues downstream, offering great views of the river as it goes.

Eventually the trail swings away from the river and moves onto the floodplain as it approaches a key **intersection (11)** in the Medlock Bridge trail system. This intersection is significant because it's one of the gateways to the unit's interior trails. It's easily identified by a large "RIVER REGULATIONS" sign on the far side of a wide and level cross trail. Turning right at that point takes you along the interior edge of the floodplain and toward that **gate (19)** you passed as you drove in on the access road, while going straight (through a small dogleg) takes you to the interior trails. For now, to continue the riverside trail, turn left.

The riverside trail swings back toward the river and remains more or less level for another 100 paces, eventually bringing you to a set of **two large timber steps (12)** on the left leading down toward the river. The main trail continues, however, swinging away from the river again as it begins to climb toward **intersection 13.** At that intersection, a right turn takes you uphill and puts you on the interior trails. The riverside trail continues straight ahead.

Beyond that intersection, the trail descends through a rooty stretch. Watch your footing. Ignore the faint spur leading off to the left.

You'll soon come to a small **bridge (14)** that crosses a little creek channel. Immediately across the bridge a set of **steep timber steps (15)** ascends and curves left. How many steps are there? Depending on whether you count roots as steps, the number may be around 20 or more.

Beyond the steps, the trail continues downstream but is now

This trailhead, to the right (upstream) of the unit's boat ramp, provides access to a very interesting riverside trail.

some distance above the river. You'll soon go around the rootball a large fallen tree. Just beyond the rootball a faint and overgrown spur drops steeply downhill, but – you guessed it – ignore the spur and stay on the main trail.

The trail climbs, then descends, and then comes to a **second set of steps (16)** which help you descend to another creek crossing. Beyond the creek you climb again, coming eventually to a brush pile on the left and just beyond it a **split in the trail (17).** The two sections of trail rejoin about 40 paces farther on.

At this point you're nearing the Medlock Bridge Unit property boundary. About 60 yards beyond the point where the split trail comes together again, a short spur goes right and uphill but quickly onto private land. Ahead, just beyond that point, a second short spur goes left toward the river. And just beyond that, at a small creek, a large POSTED sign marks the **end of the Medlock Bridge Unit (18).** It's time to turn around and backtrack to explore the unit's interior trails.

The interior trails

The third hiking opportunity at Medlock Bridge centers on the unit's network of interior trails. Accessible from the riverside trail via **intersection 11 or 13**, or from the entry road near the **gate (19)** that you passed on the way in, these trails traverse ridges, slopes, and river floodplain edges and can add a great deal of variety to any Medlock Bridge hiking experience.

One good hike in this area is a clockwise loop beginning and ending at that gate. This loop includes a section of the riverside trail and gives you a taste of everything that Medlock Bridge trails have to offer.

From the parking area, hike along the access road to the **gate (19).** , There, as you're facing the gate from the road, you'll see two wood posts to the left of the gate and, to the right of the gate, another **trailhead (24)** at the beginning of a path that goes up the hill to the right of the gate. This loop will begin at the wood posts to the left of the gate and end at the **trailhead to its right (24)**.

Passing between the timber posts puts you on a wide and well-defined trail that goes generally south as it follows the toe of an increasingly steep slope rising off to your right. About 20 yards beyond the posts note an **intersection (20)** with a trail going off the right, but continue straight ahead on the main trail.

You'll soon see a prominent **rocky bluff (21)** rising to your right. Cliffs such as this one created overhangs which the area's earliest inhabitants used as shelters, and such shelters are scattered through many of the CRNRA units.

Continue beyond the rock cliffs to **intersection 11.** Go straight through the intersection, which puts you temporarily on the riverside trail. You'll pass those two large **timber steps (12)** leading down to the river and then, beyond them, you'll come to **intersection 13.**

While hiking the riverside trail, you continued straight ahead at this intersection. But to explore the interior trails, turn right. You'll immediately begin a moderate ascent which continues for about 150 paces. The trail then turns right

One place to begin the interior loop hike is near the metal gate along the main entry drive. Start at the two wood posts to the left of the gate.

and follows the ridge north and east to another **intersection (22).** At that point the trail forks; take the left fork, which continues along the ridge for a while before beginning a descent that drops through a beautiful hollow. The trail eventually ends just a few yards from where you started – at that **trailhead to the right of the gate (24).**

What if you take the right fork at intersection 22? That puts you heading generally east on a connector trail that eventually carries you to the riverside trail at intersection 11. Along the way you'll come to an **intersection (23)** with a less-used trail that goes off to the left and toward **intersection 20** near the gate where you started, but for now stay on the main trail as it continues to head downhill. This trail becomes

A trail's eye view of intersection 11, a jumping-off point for the unit's interior trails. Here's how the intersection appears when looking away from the river toward the interior of the unit.

increasingly steep as it goes, and the last few dozen yards are *very* steep. Take your time, and proceed carefully. Just a few yards beyond the end of the descent you'll rejoin the riverside trail at **intersection 11;** the RIVER REGULATIONS sign will be on your left as you do.

What if you go left at **intersection 23?** That intersection is a little hard to see if you're coming down from up on the ridge; if you're coming up from the riverside trail, spotting it can be downright difficult. But it marks one end of the last part of the Medlock Bridge trail system, and it's definitely worth looking for.

Making the turn at intersection 23 puts you on a less-traveled but still easy to follow trail that soon climbs a bit to follow a ridgeline. It's beautiful hiking, especially in the fall. Eventually this trail traverses the *top* of those high **rocky cliffs (21)** that you saw earlier. Seeing those cliffs from below is impressive, but looking out from the top of them is an interesting experience and definitely worth doing – especially when the leaves are off the trees.

Beyond the high portion over the top of the cliffs, the trail trends to the right as it descends back toward the floodplain. It soon brings you to **intersection 20,** where you can turn left and hike a couple of dozen yards to return to your starting point near the gate at point 19.

Jones Bridge

No matter how many times you hike here, one question always remains: Where's the rest of the bridge?

The central feature of CRNRA's Jones Bridge Unit is, as you might expect, Jones Bridge.

Well, that's not exactly true. The central feature is really just *half* the bridge. So where's the other half? That's a good question.

In the early 19th century, John Martin bought land on both sides of the river (and in two counties, which becomes significant) and operated a ferry there. It was first called Martin's Ferry but eventually became known as Jones Ferry.

In 1904 a bridge was built to replace the ferry. It was welcomed by the folks who lived in the area. But the bridge suffered the ravages of time and weather, and by the 1930s it had become unsafe. Neither county wanted to cover the needed repairs, and so the bridge was eventually closed.

Today, you can still see the steel framework of *half* the bridge. It's on the Fulton County side just upriver from the unit's main parking area. The spidery remains, rusted and aging, seem to float out over the water – and then they simply stop halfway to the other side.

What happened to the other half of the bridge?

The story is that sometime in the 1940s, people began to notice workers cutting up and removing sections of the old bridge. Every-

---

Finding the trailhead:

From GA 400: Take the Ga. 140 (Holcomb Bridge Road) exit and go east for about 4.3 miles to Barnwell Road. Turn left on Barnwell Road. Then go 1.6 miles to the Jones Bridge Unit entry, which will be on your right.

---

one assumed that the work was official. But it turns out that the folks taking the bridge apart were actually *stealing* it, probably to sell as scrap metal. They got away with half the bridge, too, but the other half remains there today.

The bridge loop hike

This unit offers two major hiking opportunities. One is a fairly short hike upriver from the main parking area to the remains of the old bridge. The other is a much more ambitious hike downriver; this hike includes floodplain hiking as well as upland hiking (and of course the requisite climbing in between).

Most hikers begin here with a hike to the bridge itself. From the **main entry (1)** off Barnwell Road, go about a mile to the primary parking area at road's end. On the way you'll pass a smaller parking area at the unit's **boat ramp (2)**, but continue all the way to the main parking area at the end of the road.

The loop hike begins at the informational signs near the river end of the parking area. To your left is a **restroom building (3)**. Ahead, a short connector trail takes you to an **intersection (4)** with the main riverside trail. Turn left to begin the bridge loop hike, following the river upstream.

About 350 paces brings you to a popular **fishing platform (5)** built out into the river. Anglers enjoy fishing for trout in the deep run beyond the platform.

To your left a **utility clearing (6)** stretches back toward the restroom building and provides an alternate way back to the parking area.

Continuing upriver, you'll soon cross a **rocky area (7)** followed by more typical riverside trail. Look for an **intersection with a connector trail (8)** that forks to the left; about 20 yards beyond it a **footbridge (9)** carries you over Malvern Creek. A faint path just beyond the end of the bridge goes left. Stay on the main trail.

Anglers cast a line for some Chattahoochee trout from the fishing platform near the ruins of Jones Bridge.

Beyond the bridge look for a **canoe launch (10)** on the right. Then look to your left to see what's left of **Jones Bridge (11)**. It's an intriguing structure and a great place for photos. Note that signs warn against climbing on the ruins.

To continue the loop, pick up a trail that moves away from the river near the bridge. It eventually fords Malvern Creek. Beyond the ford, at **intersection J1,** a connector turns left toward the riverside trail. But stay on the main trail. It goes into the woods and then climbs steadily for several hundred yards before begin-

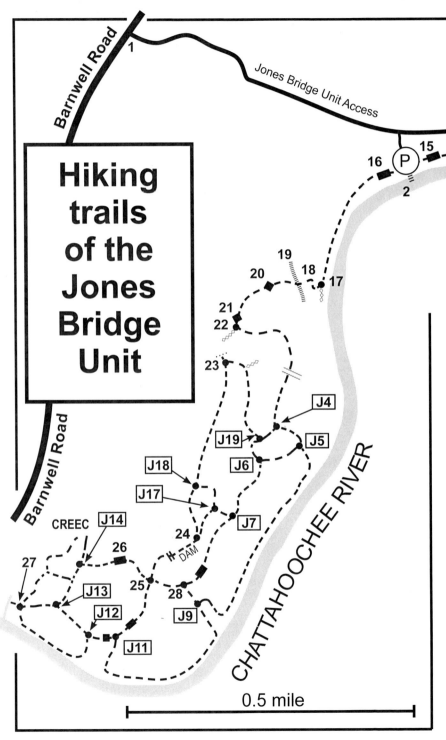

Hiking trails of the Jones Bridge Unit

CHATTAHOOCHEE RIVER

0.5 mile

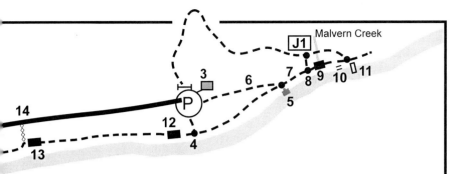

ning a long descent toward the parking area. The descent finally ends at a gate near the back of the main parking area, completing the bridge loop hike.

The south-end trails

A more ambitious Jones Bridge Unit adventure is to hike to the south end, which carries you far downriver and over an even wider variety of terrain. South-end hiking begins with a long trail that first follows the river but then swings away to climb and bypass some private land. Beyond that trail lies a network of interconnected trails that can give you hours of enjoyable walking.

From the parking area, follow the connector to **intersection 4** and turn right (downriver). About 50 paces brings you to the first **footbridge (12)** on this portion of the trail; the **next bridge (13)** awaits about 600 yards farther on.

Beyond that second bridge, you'll come to an intersection where a **spur trail cuts over to the road (14)**. The main trail turns left and continues downriver.

You'll eventually cross another **bridge (15)**. Beyond it is the unit's main **boat ramp (2)** and its parking area. This is a very small parking area, and note that some spaces may be restricted to vehicles with boat trailers. Read the signs carefully to avoid a ticket for parking in the wrong place at the wrong time.

The trail re-enters the woods across the parking area, and you'll immediately cross a neat **cable-supported footbridge (16)**. Soon you'll notice rocks on the hillside to your right. Then, a bit further, the **trail forks (17)**. The main trail (clearly delineated by timbers set in the ground) goes right. The left fork quickly comes to a private property sign. Take the right fork and stay on the main trail.

The trail soon climbs up a **switchback (with the help of some steps) (18)** and then levels before dropping sharply to cross a **gravel road (19)**. The trail continues directly across the road, crossing a **tiny footbridge (20)** and then beginning a long run to another **footbridge (21)** and, beyond it, to **intersection 22**. Go left at intersection 22 to stay on the main trail, which takes you toward **intersection J4**. You'll be traversing rolling terrain, crossing a wet-weather creek and, a bit farther along, a power line clearing. Beyond the clearing it's smooth sailing to J4, which marks the end of the connector portion of this hike and the beginning of the south-end trail network.

Incidentally, note that a faint spur trail turns right and goes uphill from intersection 22. That spur continues for about 100 yards, ending near the park boundary. To be sure that you don't stray off NPS land, stay on the main trail at

Hiker Cristina McDougal (accompanied by Casio the dog) crosses the foot bridge just south of the Jones Bridge boat ramp.

intersection 22 – in other words, go left toward J4.

The south-end loop

The south-end trails offer a spiderweb of interconnecting paths, allowing for a huge number of possible routings. Every hiker will quickly come up with personal favorites. However, one hike that many enjoy is a loop hike around the perimeter of the south-end trail complex. This guide will describe a counter-clockwise trip around that loop, beginning at **J4**.

At J4, turn right and follow a short connecting trail toward nearby **intersection J19.** Turn right again at J19 and head up the hill toward **point 23.** Along the way you'll cross several old terraces – relics from a time when farmers terraced land to make farming possible on steep terrain. You'll also pass a spur trail which leads to the right toward the powerline clearing.

The view looking downstream from the boat ramp. It's a great view at any time, but in the spring and fall it's spectacular.

40

You'll soon arrive at **point 23**. There, the main trail bends back to the left, while a short spur goes about 40 paces to a row of four timber posts that are labelled as marking the park boundary. The spur you saw earlier connects this location to point 22, but if you explore it be sure to stay on park service land.

To continue the loop, ignore the spur and go to the left on the main trail. You'll eventually descend over more terraces to **intersection J18** and, beyond it, to **point 24** and one end of a long earthen **dam**. The trail travels the length of the dam, then crosses a concrete spillway and continues on to **intersection 25**.

Turn right at intersection 25 to continue the loop. You'll follow a pleasantly wooded trail section and cross another **bridge (26)**.

Soon after that bridge the trail enters a large clearing and may become less distinct. But don't give up. On the far side of the clearing you'll eventually rejoin the loop trail (in the form of a woods road that goes right and left) near **intersection J14**. To the right is the Chattahoochee River Environmental Education Center (CREEC), which is not generally open to the public. To the left the loop hike continues, taking you toward **intersection J13** and then left again toward **intersection J12**.

If time allows you may want to explore the trails west of J13 and J12. Turning right at J13, for example, takes you toward the river and **point 27**. A bridge once crossed the creek near there, but it's now gone and has not been replaced as of this writing.

To continue the loop, go left at **J12** toward **intersection J11**. You'll cross a bridge, and then you're at J11. Going left at J11 puts you on a pleasant trail that crosses a boardwalk on its way to point 25. But turn right to continue the loop on a very scenic section of riverside trail that continues for about a quarter mile before turning inland toward **intersection J9**.

At J9, going straight leads to an intersection at **point 28**. Turning left there takes you back into the south-end trail network. Turning right takes you across a bridge and then to **J7 (**where you can turn left and climb a steep trail to **J17)** and then, beyond J7, on to **J6/J5/J4/J19**. Those four intersections form a sort of hiker's "roundabout" that lets you head off in a number of different directions.

But those are sidetrips. To continue the main loop, turn right at J9 toward **intersection J5**. The trail soon rejoins the river for a nice run of riverside hiking.

At J5, a left turn puts you on a connector that crosses the floodplain to **J6**. As you explore here, look for enigmatic piles of rocks along this connector. Can you figure out what they might be? But go right at J5 (toward **intersection J4)** to continue the loop – and when you reach J4 the loop is complete.

As you can see, the south-end trails at Jones Bridge offer a lot of options – so many that it's easy to lose track of time. That brings up a final consideration that you need to keep in mind when hiking here: When you're hiking the trails of the south end of the Jones Bridge Unit, remember that you're a *long* ways from the unit's main parking area. Be sure to leave yourself enough time to hike out and return to your car before it gets dark.

Hiker David Reyes at one of the ancient rock shelters that can be found along the riverside trail.

Island Ford

If you'll listen carefully as you hike the trails of Island Ford, you may hear ancient rock shelters whispering stories of the past.

The Island Ford Unit offers extensive and diverse hiking opportunities ranging from easy strolls to more ambitious and challenging leg-stretchers. Along the way you'll find scenic ridges, inviting creek hollows, spectacular river view, and even a chance to see a number of ancient rock shelters used by the area's earliest inhabitants.

These hiking guides will start at the south end of the unit with the trails nearest the CRNRA visitor center, starting with the boat ramp/visitor center hike. We'll then move north, looking at the lake loop hike, the riverside rock shelter trail, and the northern interior loop and Summerbrook Creek connector hikes.

We'll then go further north and explore the

Finding the trailhead:

From GA 400: Take Exit 6 (Northridge Road). Coming from the south, stay in the right lane when you exit, then cross the bridge and turn right onto Dunwoody Place. Coming from the north, continue straight at the end of the ramp onto Dunwoody Place.

Once on Dunwoody Place, go 0.5 miles to Roberts Drive. Turn right and go another 0.7 miles. The park entrance will be on your right.

north trails, accessible from the parking lot near the main entry off Roberts Road.

The boat ramp/visitor center hike

Many visitors start with the trails around the CRNRA visitor center. From the **main entry off Roberts Road (1)**, drive to the **visitor center (2)**. Once the summer home of Atlanta lawyer Samuel Hewlett, it was built in the late 1930s

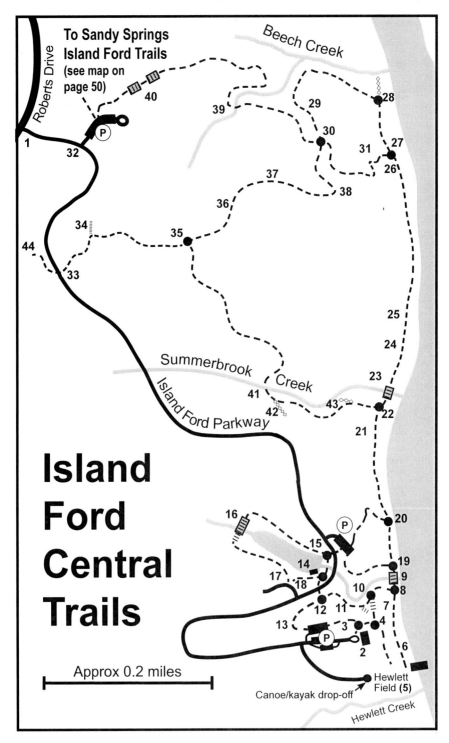

To Sandy Springs
Island Ford Trails
(see map on page 50)

Beech Creek

Roberts Drive

40

1
32

39
29
30
31
28
27
26

37
36
35
38

34
44
33

25
24

Summerbrook Creek
23

Island Ford Parkway
41
42
43
22
21

Island Ford Central Trails

16
15
14
17
18
12
13
11
10
20
19
9
8
7
4
3
2
6

P

Approx 0.2 miles

Hewlett Field (5)
Canoe/kayak drop-off

Hewlett Creek

and early 1940s using cypress logs from the Okefenokee and rock from nearby Stone Mountain. It's one of the few Adirondack-style structures in the south.

Follow the paved trail that heads downhill along the left side of the structure. You'll soon see an intersection **(3)** with a connector trail that goes left toward the parking area, but continue down the hill on the paved path. Beyond that is another **intersection (4)** with a trail that turns left, passes through a picnic area, and descends several steps to **intersection 10**. Again, stay on the concrete path as it swings right and downhill. It eventually ends near **Hewlett Field (5)**, a large grassy area. Nearby is the Island Ford boat ramp, popular with kayakers and rafters, and some picnic tables – including one right at the boat ramp.

Continue your hike on the **dirt trail (6)** that begins close to the river near

the boat ramp. You'll soon come to a fence on the river side of the trail; just beyond it look for the **large rock outcrop (7)** on your left. At the top of that outcrop is the group shelter picnic area.

The trail continues to **intersection 8** and, beyond it, a **footbridge (9)**. That bridge is the gateway to most of the Island Ford trail system. But don't cross yet. Turn left instead onto a creekside trail which leads

The CRNRA visitor center is housed in an Adirondack-style building dating from the late 1930s and early 1940s.

to **intersection 10** and wood-framed steps (32 of 'em) leading up to the picnic area above the rock outcrop.

Continue straight on the main trail. A low stone wall soon appears on the right side of the trail. Look left in that area for an **old stone spring house (11)**.

Beyond the spring house you'll climb to **intersection 12,** where a left turn puts you on a **looping trail (13)** to the lower parking area near the visitor center. If you turn right you'll soon come to Island Ford Parkway, where wood steps leads down to the road. Crossing the road puts you on the Lake Loop trail.

The lake loop

Island Ford's lake loop trail is a scenic pathway going around (you guessed it) Island Ford Lake. There are two ways to access the loop. One is to start at the visitor center and make your way to **intersection 12,** then cross the road to access the loop near a **fishing platform (14)**.

The loop is also accessible from a parking area near the lake off Island Ford Parkway. From that parking area, a trail and steps lead down toward the road. Once across, descend a few more steps and pick up the loop at **intersection 15.**

You can follow this loop in either direction. This guide starts at the fishing platform and goes counter-clockwise. From the fishing platform, walk more or less north along the

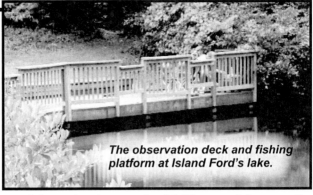

The observation deck and fishing platform at Island Ford's lake.

dam, between the dam and the road, to **intersection 15.** There, go left on a trail that moves into the woods parallel to the lakeshore.

That trail follows the lake's shoreline. Moving slowly and quietly, you may spot numerous bird species, including a variety of woodland birds as well as waterfowl on the lake and wading birds in the shallows. Also look for small animals in the woods. Deer are common, and you'll spot a turkey now and then.

Near the upper end of the lake the trail swings left to a **wooden boardwalk (16)** which carries you across a wetland and over a creek. At the end of the boardwalk you'll climb 18 moderately steep steps and then make a 90-degree turn to the left. From that point the trail moves through fairly open forest and offers more good deer-spotting opportunities.

The trail continues through the woods for a while and then exits the woods at a **paved maintenance road (17).** You can follow that road left to rejoin Island Ford Parkway, or you can turn left on a short (about 50 yards) **connector trail (18)** which leads back to the **fishing platform (14)** where you began.

Riverside rock shelter trail

One of this unit's most fascinating hikes takes you downstream along the river to several ancient rock shelters. Native Americans frequented this area

for thousands of years before the Europeans came, especially during what's known as the Woodland period from 1000 B.C. to about 900 A.D. Those original inhabitants used these naturally occurring rocky shelters to take refuge from storms or to set up overnight camps.

How many rock shelters does

This bridge, located close to the river near the CRNRA visitor center, puts you on the riverside rock shelter trail.

CRNRA contain? You'll find 'em in several CRNRA units, and most reports put the total at about 16. But the ones along this trail at Island Ford are some of the most accessible – and they still work too.

I recall a summer afternoon many years ago. My daughter was just a little girl, and we were hiking this trail when one of northern Georgia's legendary summer thunderstorms suddenly opened up. The storm came out of nowhere, bringing with it a deluge of near-Biblical proportions. We had no rain gear – but was that an overhanging rock up ahead?

Indeed it was. In fact, it was one of the trailside rock shelters. We dashed for safety under the sheltering roof and waited out the storm in relative comfort…accompanied only by the shadows of long-ago Native Americans who might have taken refuge from some other storm under the very same rock.

"Daddy," I remember her saying, "do you think that some other daddy and some other little girl might have hidden out here a long time ago?"

"It could be," I had answered.

The other day, hiking the trail yet again but this time by myself, I thought back to that day. The child is grown now and living far away. But I had one thing that those Native Americans did not have – a cell phone – and I decided that my return to that rock shelter was a

Hiker Susan Talgo, with Cassie the Labrador retriever, takes a break under another of Island Ford's rock shelters.

perfect excuse to give Daughter of Mine a call.

So I did. I told her where I was, and she instantly remembered too.

"Aw, Dad, that's sweet that you called me from there!" she said.

To hike the rock shelter trail, begin at the main parking area adjacent to the visitor's center and make your way to **intersection 8** and **foot bridge (9)**. Cross the bridge. Hike past an **intersection (19)** with a connector leading to the parking area near the lake, and continue past an **intersection (20)** with yet another (but rougher) connector leading to that same parking area. This second one seems to be used primarily by fishermen.

Roughly 250 yards beyond that second connector is the **first of the rock shelters (21)**. It's on the left side of the trail, tucked up among the trees, and an inviting little side trail beckons you to check it out.

Just beyond that shelter the trail forks at **intersection 22**. The left fork follows Summerbrook Creek upstream, eventually fording the creek and taking off uphill into the heart of the Island Ford unit. But remain on the main trail There are more rock shelters to discover!

The main trail continues on, carrying you to the **bridge (23)** over Summerbrook Creek and then to the **second rock shelter (24).** This shelter, too, invites exploration, as does a **third shelter (25)** located about 65 paces down the trail.

Beyond that third shelter, the trail continues along the river for quite a while. Eventually, close to 500 yards past the third shelter, is **rock shelter number four (26).** Literally right beside the trail, it's the one where my daughter and I took refuge that rainy day many years ago. No climbing at all is required to explore it, making it a great place to visit even with young kids.

From that point, there are two ways to complete this hike. One is to simply backtrack to the visitor's center. But if you're up for more and don't mind a section of fairly rough trail, you can complete this hike by adding a loop at the end.

Here's how to add the loop. Just past that last rock shelter is **intersection 27** where a connector trail swings left while the main trail goes straight along the river. Continue straight to **intersection 28.** There, a spur trail goes right. But go on the main trail, which soon begins to follow Beech Creek upstream

The main trail eventually swings away from the creek and begins a long and **rough climb (29).** Watch your footing! The challenging ascent continues for about 250 paces, bringing you at long last to an **intersection (30)** with a cross trail. Turning right or going straight take you onto Island Ford's interior trails, but turning left allows you to loop back to the riverside trail – so turn left.

You'll immediately ascend six wood-and-earth steps. Beyond them, a pleasant trail climbs gently for about 35 paces, then begins a long descent. Along the way a wooden boardwalk carries you over a small draw; not far beyond the boardwalk, more wood steps helps you navigate a steep section.

Beyond the steps, a series of **switchbacks (31)** carries you down toward the river, connecting with the riverside trail at **intersection 27.** At that point, turn right to return to the visitor center.

By the way, you should note that some maps show another trail swinging away from the riverside trail just south of the fourth rock shelter. That trail has been allowed to return to a natural state and is no longer available to hikers.

The northern interior loop

The Island Ford interior loop trail is especially nice on those wonderfully cool days of spring or fall. You can combine it with a hike along the riverside rock shelter trail, or you can access it via the Summerbrook Creek connector. But the easiest way to explore this loop is to begin and end at the first parking area off Island Ford Road. That's what we'll do here, hiking counterclockwise.

From the parking area hike toward the **intersection with Island Ford Parkway (32).** Then turn left and walk along the road (watch for traffic) for about 400 paces to a **trailhead (33).**

Hikers explore the Summerbrook Creek connector trail.

To your right, across the pavement and on the west side of the road, you'll see set of wood steps that puts you on a short trail. A crosswalk has been painted on the road at that point, but the paint is faint as of this writing. Promising at first, that trail quickly ends at private property.

To the left at trailhead 33, however, you'll see the start of another trail which enters the woods on the east side of the road. This trail provides additional access to the interior trail system. At first it climbs. Then it levels out and follows a ridge for quite a ways. You may eventually see an **old spur (34)** which swings left about 150 yards from the trailhead, but stay on the main trail.

You'll soon come to **intersection 35**, passing through a cut log as you do. Turning right puts you on the Summerbrook Creek connector, but to stay on the interior loop, go left. You'll immediately pass through another cut log, then come to a series of **wooden erosion controls (36)** followed by some fairly easy and mostly downhill hiking. But the downhill run soon gives way to a relatively **rough and rocky climb (37)** that continues for more than 200 yards to a point where the **trail swings distinctly left (38)**. That's where a now-abandoned and long-gone connector trail (still shown on some maps) used to begin.

You'll climb a bit, then briefly level out before making a steep descent to a **four-way intersection (30)**. To continue the loop, go left (away from the steps). The trail gently climbs and descends as you move toward a **creek crossing (39)**.

Beyond the creek crossing, the trail turns right, then soon swings left and begins a gentle ascent. It eventually brings you to two seemingly random sections of wood rail fence – one on the left side of the trail and one just beyond it on the right. Then, not quite 300 yards beyond the end of the last section of fence, you'll traverse **two wood boardwalks (40)**. A short distance beyond the last one is the parking lot where you began.

Summerbrook Creek connector

The final Island Ford trail to explore is the Summerbrook Creek connector. Access this trail either from the southern portion of the loop just described (at **intersection 35)** or from the main riverside trail via **intersection 22.** This guide will start at intersection 35 where the Summerbrook Creek connector trail intersects the interior loop described in the previous section.

From intersection 35, turn onto the connector. You'll enjoy a couple of

48

hundred yards of fairly level hiking followed by a rocky stretch and then a long descent toward the **ford over Summerbrook Creek (41)**. Just beyond the creek a **spur trail (42)** leads off up a hillside to the right, but stay on the main trail.

A few dozen yards beyond the creek crossing, you'll notice that portions of this trail are suddenly some distance *above* the creek, with a sharp drop-off toward the creek some distance below. In some places the trail is *very* close to the edge! Use extreme caution along those sections of trail.

About 120 paces beyond the creek crossing , a path turns left off the trail and leads back up the creek to one of the most interesting features of this trail – a **rock shelter (43)** that sits right beside the flowing water. You crossed the top of this rock shelter as you negotiated that rugged section of trail a few minutes earlier. Most hikers find this to be a particularly scenic shelter, and it's a big one too. Be careful of your footing if you choose to explore this area, however, for many of the rocks in the area are loose and/or slick.

Beyond the shelter, about 100 yards of easy hiking takes you back to the **intersection with the riverside trail (22)**. Turn right to return to the visitor center.

Island Ford Sandy Springs Trail

The parking lot (32) on Island Ford Parkway nearest the Roberts Drive main entry provides access to the interior loop trails, as already noted. But it also provides access to the Island Ford Sandy Springs Trail.

The Island Ford Sandy Springs Trail is a recent addition to the CRNRA suite of trails. It provides trail access to a parcel of CRNRA land not directly connected to the rest of the Island Ford Unit. Consisting of an in-and-out trail with a loop trail at the far end, these trails begin on CRNRA land, then cross property owned by the city of Sandy Springs before re-entering CRNRA holdings.

To explore these trails, begin at the first **parking area** just off Island Ford Parkway. In the parking area, look to the left for a **large white sign (44)** identifying the "Sandy Springs Island Ford Trail." An NPS info sign is there, too, as is (as of this writing) a single picnic table. The trailhead is immediately to the right of that sign. Don't confuse this trailhead with a second trailhead located a short distance to

Here's the Island Ford Sandy Springs Trail trailhead. The trail begins just to the right of the rightmost sign.

49

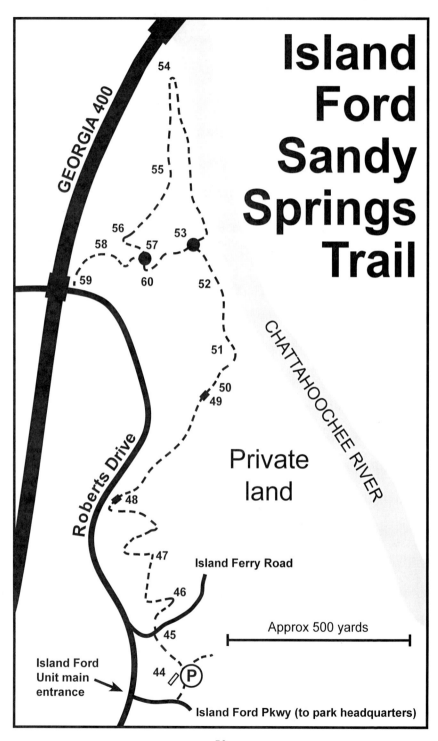

Island Ford Sandy Springs Trail

GEORGIA 400

CHATTAHOOCHEE RIVER

Private land

Roberts Drive

Island Ferry Road

Approx 500 yards

Island Ford Unit main entrance

Island Ford Pkwy (to park headquarters)

P

54
55
56
57
53
58
60
52
59
51
50
49
48
47
46
45
44

the right; that second trailhead leads into the interior loop trails described earlier.

From the trailhead, begin your hike on the in-and-out portion of this trail by following the well-defined route for about 150 yards to **the point where it crosses Island Ferry Road (45).** You'll see five large rocks blocking the trail at the road crossing. To the left, that road connects with Roberts Drive. To the right, it leads to private property.

To continue, cross Island Ferry Road and pick up the trail on the other side. Note that the trail is offset very slightly to the right on the far side of the road.

Beyond the road, another 150 paces or so will bring you through a gentle descent and to the first **switchback (46)**. Once through the switchback, you'll climb gently and the trail will turn right. It then continues to climb as you approach a high spot and yet **another switchback (47)** and a distinct left turn in the trail. A house will be visible through the trees to your right.

The trail now heads generally west. Soon it turns sharply to the right, and then (a bit further along) turns equally sharply left. You may hear the sound of automobile traffic off to your left. Also look for the tiny wet weather creek to the right of the trail. It's a good wildflower area in the spring.

The trail soon bends right again, crossing a low spot. Beyond the bend is a **wood footbridge (48)** over a wet area. As you approach this little crossing, note that the first couple of feet of the walkway are an incline. Coming from this direction, you'll see that incline as you approach. But from the other direction it's not immediately apparent. Be careful on the incline – especially if it's wet.

The trail continues relatively straight for several hundred yards, soon bringing you to a **boardwalk and wood bridge (49).** This structure begins with a short wood boardwalk and ends with an even shorter section with handrails.

At this point you're nearing the river. Look for a **rocky area (50)** on your right as you come at last to the river's floodplain. Also note the **high and rocky hillside (51)** rising off to your left – and look for your first glimpse of the Chattahoochee through the trees in front of you.

The trail climbs and descends a bit, crossing some areas that may be wet if it's recently rained. On your right the river will be visible through the trees, while more rocky hillside rises off to your left. Some of the outcrops are impressive. In particular, look for a **small shelter-like overhang (52)** not quite 200 paces beyond the point where the trail turned left to follow the river.

About 100 yards beyond the rock outcrop is an **intersection (53)** with the loop portion of this trail. The loop can be traversed in either direction; this guide will go counterclockwise, so turn right at intersection 53. You'll find yourself paralleling the river on a trail that eventually begins to traverse a natural levy separating the river on your right from a low area on your left. The vegetation here is thick, especially during the warm months. It can be another great area for wildlife and wildflowers. Note that as you near the far end of the loop, you'll cross areas that can be muddy and slippery at times.

At this point you're nearing the **sharp switchback (54)** that marks the far end of the loop. The sound of traffic on nearby Georgia 400, which has been your companion for a while now, is more noticeable here.

Make the sharp left turn at the switchback to begin your return. The trail will immediately begin to climb. Steep at first, the ascent soon moderates as the trail finds its place on the flank of the ridge and begins to head back in the general direction from which you came. The trail you came in on will be visible below you, only a short distance away horizontally but farther and farther away vertically as you generally continue to climb.

Just beyond a short **rocky section (55)**, the trail swings right away from the river as it continues through a series of fairly gentle ascents and descents. You'll soon come to a **stone crossing over a wet-weather branch (56).** Then, not

far beyond that crossing, you'll come to an **intersection (57)** with a trail which gently climbs to the right.

That right-turning trail is actually a fairly short **spur trail (58)** which leads to Roberts Drive very near the point where it passes beneath Georgia 400. It goes to Roberts Drive and stops. At one point along the way, the trails seems to be taking you directly toward Georgia 400. In fact, you'll see and hear the Georgia 400 traffic as it zips by straight in front of you – an oddly disconcerting experience after an hour or more of hiking in the woods!

Hikers enjoy the Island Ford Sandy Springs trail.

Soon, this connecting spur **ends at Roberts Drive (59).** Note that there is only a trailhead at that point; there is no parking at that location. The unmarked Roberts Drive trailhead is located to the *right* of a utility pole (it's pole number N2065, to be precise). Note that the trailhead here is *not* the brown swinging gate just to the left of the pole. It's the foot path to the *right* of the pole.

From Roberts Drive, backtrack to rejoin the main loop at **intersection 57.** Turn right at that point to continue the loop. You'll **cross another wet weather branch (60)** on another stone crossing. Beyond it, the trail swings left. You'll soon cross another tiny wet-weather branch; look for the rocks along the trail to your right just beyond this crossing. The trail then begins a gentle descent back to **intersection 53,** where you can turn right to return to the parking area or go straight to hike the loop again.

Trout Fishing
in the
Hooch

As you hike Island Ford and many other CRNRA units, you'll probably see fishermen trying their luck in the river. Most of them are trout fishermen, pursuing the rainbow and brown trout for which this section of river is widely known.

The river below Buford Dam wasn't always a trout fishery, however. Before the construction of the dam it was a "warmwater" river – that is, one with water too warm to support the cold-loving trout. However, when Buford Dam was closed to create Lake Lanier in 1957, a 40-plus mile stretch downriver from the dam became a "coldwater" river. The reason? Water is discharged into the river from the bottom of the lake, and that water is *cold!*

At first the Chattahoochee's potential as a trout river was not recognized. However, the story you hear is that in 1959 a group of Atlanta anglers covertly stocked a section with trout...and then, once the trout had become established, they invited state wildlife officials to sample the fishing. The officials were impressed and eventually launched an ongoing trout stocking program that continues today. There's even natural trout reproduction in some sections of the river.

Chattahoochee trout anglers use all sorts of fishing techniques, and you'll see fishermen using everything from fly rods to spinning rods to cane poles as they pursue these hard-fighting fish. Be sure to check license requirements and current fishing regulations for different sections of the river; you can access the latest regulations at **www.gofishgeorgia.com**.

There are many resources that will help you learn more about trout fishing in the Chattahoochee. One is North Georgia Trout Online (**www.ngto. org**), where you'll find helpful folks eager to answer your questions. Another good resource is one of the many Trout Unlimited chapters in the area; you can find contact info for Trout Unlimited chapters throughout the area by visiting **www.tu.org** and going to the "Chapter/ Council Contacts" tab.

Vickery Creek

You'll find some great hiking (and some fascinating history too) along the trails of Vickery Creek

This nineteenth-century mill dam still stands on Vickery Creek.

Vickery Creek is said to be named for a Cherokee woman, Vickery, on whose land the creek began. She was forced west on the infamous Trail of Tears, but her name remained as the name of the creek. Later, settlers began calling it "Big Creek," and you'll hear it referred to by both names today. In the interest of history, we'll call it Vickery Creek here.

Vickery Creek was made to order for water power. The terrain is ideal for

Finding the trailheads:

From GA 400: Take the Northridge Road exit (Exit 6). At the end of the ramp, turn west on Northridge Rd. Go to Highway 9/Roswell Road and turn right (north). Cross the Chattahoochee. You'll immediately come to the intersection with Riverside Road/Azalea Drive. Then...

To reach the main Riverside Road parking area (point 1): At the light at that intersection, turn right on Riverside Road. Cross Vickery (Big) Creek and make an immediate left into the parking area.

To reach the Allenbrook parking area (point 2): At the light at that intersection, stay straight (on South Atlanta Road). Look for the right turn into the Allenbrook parking area about a quarter mile beyond the light. Watch carefully, as this entrance will sneak up on you.

Other parking possibilities: You can park at Roswell's Old Mill Park, near the new covered bridge **(point 45)**, and cross that bridge to access the Vickery Creek Unit trails. There's also limited parking at a small lot off Oxbo Road **(point 51)**, which provides access to the Vickery Creek unit via a gravel multiuse trail and a steel pedestrian bridge over the creek.

Trails of the Vickery Creek Unit

Approx 0.3 miles

This map and the accompanying hike descriptions focus on trails within CRNRA. Trails outside CRNRA, including the nearby network of Roswell Historic Trails, are not detailed here.

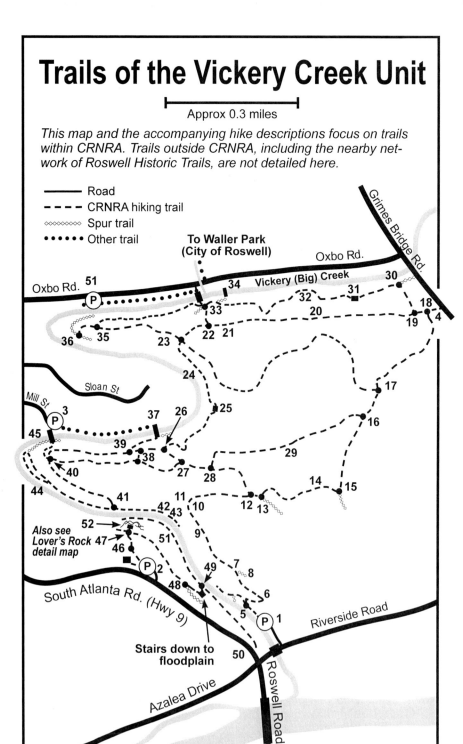

——— Road
- - - - CRNRA hiking trail
∞∞∞∞ Spur trail
•••• Other trail

To Waller Park
(City of Roswell)

Grimes Bridge Rd.

Oxbo Rd.

Oxbo Rd. 51

Vickery (Big) Creek

51 P

34 33 30

32 31

20 18

19 4

36 35 23 22 21

24

Sloan St

17

Mill St 3

45 P

37 26 25 16

39 38 29

40 27 28

44 41 11 14 15

42 43 10 12 13

52

Also see
Lover's Rock 47
detail map 46 51 9

P 2 7

48 49 8

South Atlanta Rd. (Hwy 9) 6

5 P 1

Stairs down to
floodplain 50

Riverside Road

Azalea Drive

Roswell Road

building dams – and that was good news for 19th century entrepreneur Roswell King. King developed textile mills here (and also set the stage for what would become the booming town of Roswell) beginning in the 1830s.

By the 1850s the industrial complex along Vickery Creek included not only cotton mills but also a woolen mill. Among the products produced at that woolen mill was the gray wool cloth used to make Confederate uniforms during the Civil War. That didn't sit well with Union troops, who burned not only the woolen mill but also two cotton mills.

Although the mills were destroyed, the buildings were left standing and were eventually rebuilt. Some of those 19th century structures (including the original mill dam) can still be seen today, either from the trails of Vickery Creek or from easily accessible city trails leading upstream from Roswell's Old Mill Park.

There are several access points for the Vickery Creek trails. The primary **CRNRA parking area and trailhead (1)** is off Riverside Road; it provides access to the unit's perimeter and interior trails. A second CRNRA parking area, at **Allenbrook (2),** provides access to the trails on the south side of the unit.

These trails are also accessible from Roswell's park and trail system via parking areas at Old Mill Park **(3)** and off Oxbo Road **(51).**

Finally, you can access the parks via the **trailhead off Grimes Bridge Road (4).** But note that there is no parking at that location.

The main loop hike

The Vickery Creek trails lend themselves well to a long loop hike, which starts at the **main parking area off Riverside Road (1).** Look for the trailhead at the far end of the parking area.

Follow the trail a short distance to an **intersection (5)** and a fork. The left fork goes toward Vickery Creek. Some maps still show that trail continuing upstream along the creek, but the connecting section was not safe and has been closed for some time. So turn right (uphill) at intersection 5, climbing up a set of steps and then beginning a long ascent up to higher ground. At first the trail clings to a steep slope. But it eventually makes a **hairpin bend to the left (6)** and widens to offer much better hiking.

Eventually the climb ends near a convenient **bench (7),** allowing you to pause and catch your breath – and to look out over the trees below you. You have climbed a long way! Also notice the **spur trail (8)** that begins just before the bench. Promising at first, it eventually fades away in a patch of ivy.

The main trail continues to climb. You'll eventually reach a **section of fence (9)** on the left side of the trail; it blocks off an area that's being restored. Beyond it is **a second bench (10)** and, soon after, another **fence section (11).**

You'll eventually come to an **intersection (12)** where you can go straight or left. A left takes you into the heart of the unit; to continue this loop, go straight.

About 45 paces brings you to an **intersection with a spur trail (13)** that turns right but soon ends at the park boundary. The main trail swings left, rising and

The main CRNRA Vickery Creek trailhead is located off Riverside Road near Highway 9. Just beyond the trailhead, a set of steps (below) puts you on the main Vickery Creek trail network.

falling as it goes, with one particularly **sharp but short ascent and descent (14)**.

You'll soon reach **intersection 15.** At that point, a right puts you on a short spur that soon leaves park property. Instead, go left to continue the loop on a wide trail that takes you to **intersection 16,** where you'll see a small arrow sign pointing left along a trail into the interior. But the loop continues ahead toward **intersection 17** where another interior trail turns left. Again, go straight to continue the loop.

Beyond intersection 17, the trail meanders as it heads toward Grimes Bridge Road. You'll hear traffic as you approach **intersection 18,** which is marked by no less than three NPS signs (an info sign, a regulations sign, and a trail map) and one Historic Roswell Trail System sign. Turning right at that point (toward the traffic) takes you to a **trailhead on Grimes Bridge Road (4)**. There, a single marker post identifies the trailhead, which might otherwise be lost among the roadside vegetation. There's no parking at this trailhead – only a sidewalk.

To continue the loop, go left (west) at point 18 along a relatively straight but definitely rolling section of trail. About 70 paces beyond the intersection you'll ford a small creek, but just before you do look for an **intersection (19)** with a connector trail turning right off of the main trail. It cuts over to a trail which roughly parallels Vickery Creek. We'll look more at that one in a moment.

For now, go straight and ford the creek to continue the loop. The trail moves roller coaster style to **another creek crossing (20)** followed by a steep and rooty climb. At the top you'll enjoy a stretch of easier hiking, but it soon ends in a very steep and rugged descent to **yet another creek crossing (21)**.

Beyond that last creek crossing the trail climbs to **intersection 22,** where you can turn right and descend a steep connector trail to **intersection 33.** We'll take a look at that intersection, and the possibilities it offers, momentarily. For now, however, continue the loop by going straight (west) through intersection 22. The

Here's intersection 33 (right), where the Oxbo Bridge foot bridge crosses Vickery Creek and connects the CRNRA trails with the City of Roswell's trail system.

trail will trend to the left as it approaches **intersection 23,** a very wide intersection with a cross trail. Turning right (west) puts you on a spur that follows a ridge before dropping very sharply to the creek floodplain – more about that in a minute. Turning east puts you on one of the most scenic trails in the entire unit; it winds and meanders through beautiful forest for close to three-quarters of a mile before finally ending at intersection 17.

But to continue the main loop, go straight through intersection 23. The trail descends, swings left and soon begins to follow the rocky edge of a bluff with **large outcrops of rock (24)** evident on the steep slopes and Vickery Creek flowing far below. Soon, a **footbridge (25)** carries you across a small creek; beyond it, you'll eventually reach **intersection 26.** There, to continue the loop, go left (more or less east) toward **intersection 27.** We'll look at the other options from point 26 after we finish the loop.

Continue to **intersection 28.** If you turn left (north) at that point, the trail will quickly bend to the east and eventually carry you to intersection 16 (which you encountered earlier). Along the way, look for an **old fenced area (29)** just off the trail. The trail from 28 to 16 is relatively lightly used and may be overgrown in places, so if you hike it in the summer check for ticks when you get home.

To complete the loop, go east (straight) as you approach intersection 28. That takes you back to intersection 12, where you can turn right and backtrack to the parking area off Riverside Road.

A north-end alternative

As you may have guessed by now, the main Vickery Creek loop hike bypasses some very interesting trails. Would you like to explore those too?

One option is to start back at intersection 19, where that connector trail turns right just before a creek ford. Instead of going straight toward point 22, turn right and follow the connector to **intersection 30.** From there, you can go right and follow a spur up Vickery Creek to Grimes Bridge Road...but there's no convenient access (without hopping over a concrete wall) to the sidewalk along that road. Thus, a better alternative is to turn left at intersection 30 (immediately fording a small creek) and then follow a clear trail that moves along the flank of the ridge some distance above Vickery Creek.

The trail, which includes a number of ascents and descents, continues through the woods and soon brings you to a **foot bridge (31)** over a steep-walled creek channel. Beyond the bridge the trail **fords a creek (32)** – and beyond that point it won't be long till you hear rushing water. The sound comes from water pouring over a **modern low-head dam (34),** which you can see by following a short spur that appears to your right just before the next intersection **(intersection 33).** The spur takes you to a fenced observation point near one end of the dam.

Return to the main trail and continue to **intersection 33,** which marks the other end of the steep connector you encountered back at intersection 22. Several trails radiate from that point; the most prominent curves downhill to the Oxbo Bridge, a large steel pedestrian bridge which crosses Vickery Creek to connect with the City of Roswell's multi-use trail network. A brochure describing the city's trails can be picked up at the Roswell Visitor Center.

Two other spur trails also begin here. One takes off uphill and soon fades away. But the second drops down toward the creek and goes west, climbing some distance above the creek as it moves toward **intersection 35.**

At point 35, a right turn soon brings you a steep, rocky descent which drops toward the floodplain and then **deadends at a cross trail (36).** If you turn right at that point, the trail soon crosses under a jumble of large fallen tree trunks and limbs and then parallels the creek up to the point where a large pipe crosses the creek. Just beyond that point this arm of the trail ends.

To the left of 36, a spur trail continues for a ways but can be extremely overgrown. In the summer, this section seems to be another favorite habitat for ticks.

After exploring this area, backtrack from 36 to 35 and carefully make the steep climb up the rocky section. But this time go straight through intersection 35, which puts you on a refreshingly pleasant section of trail that follows a ridge toward to point 23, your intersection with the main loop described earlier.

West of intersection 26?

Another neat sight bypassed by the main loop is the **30-foot-high stone mill dam (37)** built in the 1830s to provide water power for this area's mills. Here's how to get a close-up look at the dam. From point 26, instead of going left to hike the main loop, turn right instead. You'll pass through an intersection with a **connector trail (38)** that goes uphill. Just beyond it, at **intersection 39,** a trail turns right and downhill, leading directly to the old dam. There's even a bench just past the end of the dam, making this a favorite spot to take a mid-hike break.

After seeing the dam, return to point 39 and continue hiking west toward **intersection 40.** There, a right turn puts you on a connector that leads to the **Vickery Creek Covered Pedestrian Bridge (45)** which links Roswell's Old Mill

In many parts of the Vickery Creek Unit, Vickery (Big) Creek provides the constant sound of dancing water to accompany you as you hike.

Park with CRNRA's Vickery Creek Unit. That bridge provides another popular access point to the Vickery Creek trails; it also offers great views of the creek.

Another option from point 40 is to go straight toward **intersection 41**. Be aware that it's one long descent, and the lower portion is rutted and rocky.

What happens at intersection 41? A left turn takes you downstream along the creek, with numerous short spur trails leading to the water. You'll eventually

The Old Mill Park covered bridge provides another connection between Vickery Creek's trails and City of Roswell trails.

ford a small creek (42); beyond that point, look for large rock outcrops. And just beyond the point where the rock outcrops appear, the trail is blocked by a cable. That's the end of this trail, so backtrack to point 41.

What if you go *upstream* from point 41. In that case the trail follows the creek, eventually forking to form a **loop (44)** of sorts that provides great access to the creek. At the far end of the loop several large pipes converge at a concrete sewer manhole. An undeveloped spur trail continues upstream beyond that point, eventually passing under the covered bridge as it makes its way up the creek.

The Allenbrook trails

Most of the Vickery Creek trail system is within the area bounded by Vickery Creek. But there's also good hiking between the creek and Highway 9/South Atlanta Street. Often referred to as the "Allenbrook trails," this group of footpaths offers a unique hiking experience as well as an additional serving of history.

This area is named for the red brick structure known as "Allenbrook," built in the 1850s as residence and office for the manager of the Ivy Woolen Mill. When Union troops passed through on their way to Atlanta, the resident manager raised the French flag in an attempt to save the mills and the house. He was partially successful; Union soldiers burned the mills but left the house alone.

Allenbrook, built in the 1850s, served as office and residence for the manager of the Ivy Woolen Mill.

At this time there is no over-the-creek connection between the Vickery Creek trails and the Allenbrook trails. There's talk of building a pedestrian bridge connecting the two at some point in the future, but for now hikers have to access the

Allenbrook trails from the Allenbrook parking area, which is located directly off South Atlanta Road/Highway 9. This parking area is adjacent to historic Allenbrook, just over a quarter mile north of the light at Riverside Road/Azalea Drive. Keep a sharp eye out for the turn. You'll miss it if you're not careful. Once you make the turn off South Atlanta Road/Highway 9, follow the graveled drive to a small parking area. Beyond the parking area you'll see Allenbrook, which is currently being restored and is closed to visitors. You'll also see the trailhead at the far end of the parking area.

From the trailhead, follow a path across a grassy area. The path soon **enters the woods (46),** then

A lone hiker ascends the long run of timber steps back toward Allenbrook and the nearby parking area.

descends two long curving flights of timber-and-earth steps to **intersection 47** where you can go left, right, or straight ahead.

Most visitors want to go straight first, making their way down a run of 21 steps to a delineated (by several timbers) lookout spot at the top of **Lover's Rock (52).** This spot is also known as Lover's Leap or the Vickery Creek Overlook. From the top, Lover's Rock offers spectacular views along Vickery Creek – especially in the winter when the leaves are off the trees. Be extremely careful in this area, as there is no guardrail and the edge is closer than you think.

After checking out the overlook, climb back up to **intersection 47.** Turning right will put you on a short section of trail that quickly ends. Going left, however, begins a long and relatively gentle descent to **intersection 48.**

At intersection 48, a spur trail goes right, becomes overgrown and soon disappears. To stay on the main trail, go left and continue downhill to a set of

four flights of wooden steps which carry you over a steep section and down to the floodplain – and to **intersection 49** with the floodplain trail.

Should you go right or left at 49? Going right (downstream) puts you on a relatively lightly used trail that soon swings away from the creek and eventually ends at a map post just a few yards from the road. It's theoretically possible to access the trail at that point, but it would be difficult. Besides, there's no

Enjoying the shelter of the Lover's Rock rock shelter, arguably the most spectacular of the many CRNRA rock shelters.

sidewalk and no parking. South Atlanta Road/Highway 9 is a very busy road with narrow lanes and, in this area, no sidewalk on the Allenbrook side. It's not the place for walking.

But let's get back to the trail.

Since a right turn from intersection 49 doesn't really take you anywhere, most hikers go left (up the creek) instead. It's a nice walk along a clear trail, and it offers beautiful views of shoals along the creek.

As you continue to hike upstream, you'll soon notice **rock outcrops (51)** beginning to appear alongside the trail. The overhanging ledges provide protection from the elements, and many of them were used by the area's original inhabitants for shelter or as living space. You may also notice the rock outcrops becoming larger and more dramatic the farther along you go.

And then, suddenly, there it is – **Lover's Rock (52)** as seen from the other side.

From creek level you really get a sense of the massive scale of this sheltering outcrop. Its shelf-like overhang soars about 100 feet above the floodplain, offering shelter that was utilized by the early inhabitants of this area. It's easy to imagine them taking cover under these overhangs. It is, by almost any measure, the most spectacular of the rock shelters to be found in CRNRA – and seeing it is your reward for making it to the end of the trail.

After exploring the rock shelter, backtrack to intersection 49 and climb the steps to return to the parking area near Allenbrook.

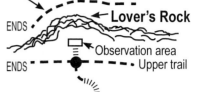

Vickery Creek

Lower (creek level) trail...a long way down

ENDS

Lover's Rock

Observation area

ENDS — Upper trail

Up steps to parking area

Detail:

Lover's Rock area

Here's a detailed overhead look at Lover's Rock. Hikers can access the top or the bottom, but the best and most impressive views are from the bottom – that is, from the lower (creek level) trail.

There are several unofficial spur trails in this area, but many of them are very steep and are potentially dangerous. The official lower trail stops at Lover's Rock and does *not* continue up the steep slope to connect with the upper trail. Don't try it.

IMPORTANT! The top of Lover's Rock is potentially dangerous. While there is a viewing area outlined on the ground at the top, near point 47, there's *no railing* around it – and the edge is closer than you think. Rocks can be slippery and footing can be unsure, even when it's dry. This is not a place for small children...or for anyone, of any age, who's inclined to be reckless or careless. Explore here solely at your own risk.

Chattahoochee Nature Center Boardwalk

The Chattahoochee Nature Center is a 127-acre environmental showcase offering a variety of educational opportunities for children and adults, all focused on the Chattahoochee River. It also offers several hiking opportunities, including the half-mile-long River Boardwalk Trail. This trail takes you through wetlands along Bull Sluice, the lake formed behind Morgan Falls Dam. Although it's not part of CRNRA, it offers a great perspective on the river and is included here.

The River Boardwalk Trail is a loop that can be hiked in either direction. Platforms along the trail provide great observation points. Waterfowl and other birds are common, and you may also see mammals including river otters, beavers, or mink.

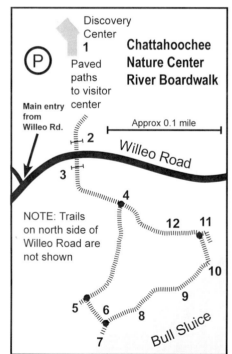

Park at the Discovery Center **visitor center (1)** and take care of the admission fee at the front desk. Then walk down the hill from the visitor center to the boardwalk trailhead across Willeo Road. A **gate (2)** allows you to pass through the fence at the road, and just beyond that gate a traffic signal control button (on your right) lets you activate the stoplight at the crosswalk. Let the light stop traffic before you cross, as the crossing is in a curve and traffic can be fast.

Once across the road you'll see the **trailhead (3)** and boardwalk directly in front of you. The boardwalk may be slippery if it's wet, so watch your footing.

You'll soon reach **intersection (4)** where the loop portion begins. This guide goes counterclockwise, so turn right at the intersection. You'll soon reach an **observation platform (5)** on your right, the first of several along the boardwalk. This one's a favorite among birdwatchers, especially during annual migrations.

Continue along the boardwalk to another **intersection (6)** and (on the right) a covered **A-frame observation area (7)** that offers great views across Bull Sluice Lake.

Beyond the A-frame, a convenient **bench (8)** provides a good place to take a break. That's followed by a post-mounted **telescope (9)** which offers a close-up look at what's going on in the wetlands. A guide attached to the telescope support describes many of the birds you're likely to see.

Finding the trailhead:

From Georgia 400, exit at Northridge Road (exit 6). Go west to Roswell Road and turn right. After crossing the Chattahoochee River, turn left onto Azalea Drive. Continue to Willeo Road (just past a bend to the left) and turn left, then continue on Willeo Road for about a half mile to the Chattahoochee Nature Center on your right.

The boardwalk soon turns left. A **plaque (10)** at that point commemorates the August 1993 naming of Atlanta's Chattahoochee River and Scotland's Tweed River as twin rivers.

Beyond the turn a short **spur (11)** goes right to a canoe launch area, and another **observation platform (12)** soon appears on your right. From there it's only a short walk back to intersection 4 and the trailhead at Willeo Road.

As of this writing the boardwalk is open Monday-Saturday from 10-5 and on Sundays from 12-5, though it may be closed during bad weather – or if it's underwater. Since the level of Bull Sluice Lake is affected by water releases from Buford Dam upstream and from Morgan Falls Dam downstream, there are indeed times when the boardwalk may be submerged.

In addition to the boardwalk, the Chattahoochee Nature Center includes several other paved and unpaved trails which you may want to check out – especially if you have the kids with you. These short paths (none more than a third of a mile in length) lead to (among other things) a beaver pond, a bald eagle aviary, traces of a 1940s cabin, and many more great wildlife observation opportunities. All in all, it's a great family destination.

A group of hikers checks out Bull Sluice Lake from one of many vantage points along the Gold Branch trail system.

Gold Branch

The trails of the Gold Branch Unit carry you pretty much out into the middle of nowhere. But isn't that why you came?

The Gold Branch Unit trails offer a distinct "backcountry" feel. If you're looking to get away from it all for a bit, these may be the trails for you.

The unit is bordered for the most part by Bull Sluice Lake, a 580-acre impoundment formed following construction of Morgan Falls Dam in 1904. Over the decades the lake has accumulated a lot of silt – so much so that many parts of it are now fairly shallow. That diminishes the lake's flood management capacity, but (on the other hand) it has created some incredible wildlife habitat.

We'll look at these trails in four sections. The first describes the connector leading from the trailhead to the main trail network. All Gold Branch hikes begin on that connector trail.

The weblike northern network trails are covered next. They can be mixed and matched to provide a variety of hiking experiences ranging from easy to hard.

Then there's the central

Finding the trailhead

From GA 400: Take Exit 6 (Northridge Road). If you're coming from the south, stay in the right lane when you exit, then cross the bridge and turn right onto Dunwoody Place. If you're coming from the north, continue straight at the end of the ramp onto Dunwoody Place.

Go 1.3 miles on Dunwoody Place, and turn right at Roswell Road. Go 0.6 miles and turn left at Azalea Drive. Then go 1.7 miles and turn left at Willeo Road. Follow Willeo Road for 1.4 miles. Then turn left at Lower Roswell Road and go another 0.7 miles to the park entrance on your left.

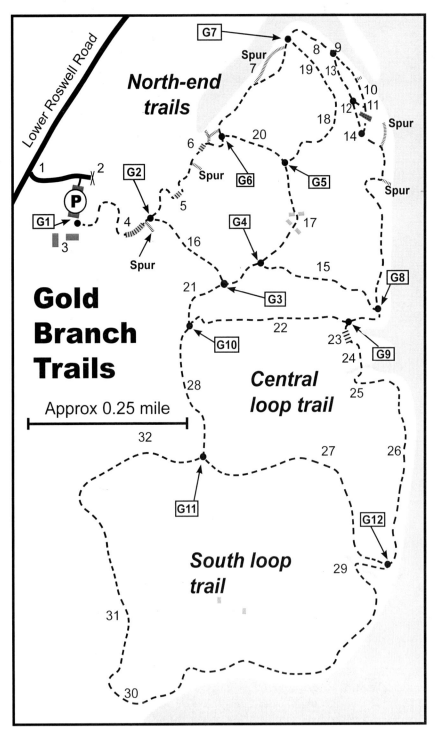

Lower Roswell Road

G7

Spur
7

8 9

19 13

**North-end
trails**

10
12 11
Spur

18

14 Spur

1 2

G2

6

20

Spur

G6

G5

P

G1

4

5

G4

17

**Gold
Branch
Trails**

3

Spur

16

15

G8

21

G3

Approx 0.25 mile

22

G10

23

G9

24

32

28

25

**Central
loop trail**

27

26

G11

G12

**South loop
trail**

29

31

30

loop – essentially an in-and-out hike with a loop at the end. It's a moderate hike that will challenge you with some long grades. But the reward for making the trek is some incredible scenery.

Finally, explore the "south loop," a relatively emote trail in the southern part of Gold Branch. Portions of this hike (in particular, the higher elevation uplands sections) offer straightforward hiking on wide and easy-to-follow trails. But other parts are much more challenging.

The trailhead is located near the parking area. Here's how it looks from in the woods just a few yards into the trail.

Thanks to several connector trails, there are many ways to combine these hikes. You can even make a big loop hike around the outermost of the unit's trails. It's a great hike – if you're up to the challenge!

The Main Access Trail

All Gold Branch hikes start at the trailhead off Lower Roswell Road. A **turnoff (1)** from Lower Roswell Road leads to a right turn into the **parking area**. Do not go straight beyond the turn, as that takes you to a **barrier gate (2)**.

This unit's parking area is worth a word or two in its own right. The parking area is paved with a special porous concrete that lets storm water percolate slowly through the concrete instead of running off all at once and potentially causing erosion or thermal shock to the Chattahoochee River.

The **trail head (G1)** is at the far corner of the parking area near several large informational signs. Behind those signs are several **picnic tables (3)**.

From the trailhead, you'll immediately enter the woods. Several wood-framed earth steps help you down a short grade. Beyond them the trail trends left and steepens as it descends toward a **boardwalk (4)** over a wetland. Just beyond the boardwalk is **intersection G2**, the jumping-off point for the Gold Branch trail system.

Going right at G2 provides the most direct access to the middle and southern portions of the unit's trails, while going left takes you to the north-end trails. Ignore the faint spur trail turning to the right at the end of the boardwalk.

The North-End Trails

The north-end trails – those trails including and north of the routes connecting intersections G2, G3, G4 and G8 – offer a variety of hiking opportunities. These trails traverse wetlands and creek valleys as well as upland forests and shoreline. They range from wide and level to narrow and steep and challenging.

We'll start with the north-end loop. From the trail head (G1), make your way to intersection G2 and go left on the main trail. It's fairly level for about 60 paces, though some sections are rooty. The trail soon trends to the right and climbs a series of rough earthen steps, followed by another run of relatively level trail and then a **wooden bridge (5)** over a creek gully.

After crossing the bridge, you'll soon come to another rooty stretch. Then – off to your left – you'll get your first good glimpse of water as you approach an arm of Bull Sluice Lake.

The trail soon begins a descent toward **another bridge (6)**. Across the bridge a spur leads to the edge of the water. Nearby, another climbs steeply from the bridge to rejoin the main trail just beyond point G6. But stay on the main trail.

Beyond the bridge the trail meanders, then climbs steeply to **intersection G6**. There you could turn right to go into the interior of the northern section, but for now go left to stay on the loop. It's "easy" trail all the way to **intersection G7**.

Note that a **side trail (7)** swings away from the main trail along this stretch, dropping down the hill to parallel (sometimes closely!) the water before rejoining the main trail a short distance before coming to intersection G7.

At G7 you could go right to explore the interior, but for now go straight to continue the loop. Soon you'll see several large rocks on the uphill side of the trail, including one **great "bench rock" (8)** that's a good place to sit and take a break.

Beyond the bench rock **the trail splits (9)**. One fork goes along the water. But the

This boardwalk, on the approach trail leading from the parking area and trailhead, takes you to intersection G2. That's the jumping-off point for hiking the Gold Branch system of trails.

69

other goes right and immediately begins to climb. Which is best? Consider the straight-ahead trail first. It continues mostly level for about 60 paces, eventually coming to an old spur trail that turns off to the left (ignore it). Just beyond the spur is about 75 paces of **very rough and very steep trail (10)** that climbs over some rugged terrain. Use extreme caution here!

The path soon makes a **sharp hairpin bend back to the right (11)** (to bypass a large downed tree which blocks the way ahead) and then comes to another **intersection (12)**. At that point, turn left to continue the loop.

Could you avoid the tough trail by taking the right fork at intersection 9? That would put you on a **very steep ascent (13)** that is, if anything, even worse than what you found along the left fork. This section of trail climbs roughly for about 90 yards. Then it levels out and begins a relatively gentle descent toward intersection 12. Beyond that is another **intersection (14)** where you could go left and, eventually, back the way you came – except for the fact that it's blocked by that large fallen tree you encountered earlier. Stay right to stay on the trail.

Continue hiking toward G8 along what's now an easy stretch of trail. Spurs go left at several points. After about a half mile you'll come to **intersection G8**. There, turn right and begin a **steady climb (15)** that continues for quite a while. The trail doesn't level out until just before you reach **intersection G4**.

To finish the loop, go left at G4 and hike about 140 yards of easy trail to G3. At G3, turn right to begin a steady, occasionally rough **descent (16)** towards G2 near the end of the boardwalk, completing the loop.

To explore the north end's interior trails, turn right instead of left at G4 toward **intersection G5**. Along the way you'll pass through **a pair of cut tree trunks (17)** that once blocked the trail. The two fallen trunks, about 25 paces apart, have been cut to allow easy passage.

At G5, going right puts you on a **trail (18)** which follows a ridgeline before beginning a fairly strenuous **descent (19)** towards intersection G7.

What if you decide to turn left at G5 and hike toward G6? That puts you on **another descending connector trail (20)** that eventually intersects the waterside trail at G6.

Clearly, there are many ways to combine the trails within the northern portion of Gold Branch. You can mix and match the individual trail sections to craft a hike of almost any length and degree of difficulty that you desire. But even with all of that north-end hiking, you're really just getting started at Gold Branch!

The central loop

A second popular route in this unit is what many call the "central loop." From intersection G2, take the right fork to explore this loop. That'll put you on a **section of trail (16)** that climbs for about a quarter of a mile, arriving finally at **intersection G3**. Turn right at that point, which puts you on a wide and easy-to-follow section of **trail (21)**. The first stretch will be fairly level, but then comes

Some sections of the Gold Branch central loop trail closely follow the edge of Bull Sluice, providing excellent opportunities to view wildlife.

about 100 paces of descending trail that calls for watching your footing. Exposed roots can trip the unwary, so use caution as you go.

You'll eventually arrive at **intersection G10** and the start of the central loop. Most hikers find this loop easier when hiked clockwise. That's the way we'll do it here, so turn left (east) at G10 and begin a long and steady descent. The trail shifts from a wide country-lane-like walkway to a **narrow and pleasantly intimate path (22)** as it makes its way down the ridge toward Bull Sluice Lake.

The gentle downhill hike is refreshing, and it eventually brings you to **intersection G9** and the edge of Bull Sluice. A left at G9 leads back to the northern loop at intersection G8, but turn right to explore the central loop.

You'll descend for several dozen yards – fairly steeply at first – and then veer right before coming to a **wooden footbridge (23)** over a small creek. Across the bridge the trail generally follows the creek downstream, then trends to the right and **fords a small creek (24)**.

Just beyond the creek, hikers used to be faced with what had come to be called "The Climb" – a root-grabbing, rock-scrambling near-vertical ascent up an extremely steep section of trail. Recently, however, the trail has been rerouted around The Climb; it now takes you around the steep section on a newly-constructed **switchback (25)** that offers much easier (and much safer) hiking.

Beyond the switchback the **trail follows the shore (26)** of Bull Sluice for several hundred yards. At first, this trail is characterized by some relatively rugged sections. But approaching **intersection G12** things begin to level out.

Turn right at G12 to continue the central loop. That puts you on a **moderately challenging section of trail (27)** that immediately dishes out a long run of steady climbing. Some subsequent descents and still more climbing delivers you at last to **intersection G11,** where you can complete the central loop hike by turning right to follow a **wide and pleasantly level trail (28)** along the ridge and back to G10. Go left at G10, then backtrack to the trailhead and parking lot.

The south loop

The last Gold Branch hike is the south loop – a sometimes remote, always fascinating loop in the southern portion of the unit. It takes you far from the beaten track, at least as CRNRA hikes go. That remoteness adds to its wilderness feel. But note that parts of this route are definitely in the "rugged" category. This is not a good trail for small children.

If you're ready for the challenge, start by hiking from the trailhead to **intersection G11**. Now should you go left or right? This guide takes you around the loop clockwise, so turn left at G11 and make your way along a **section of varied trail (27)** that carries you toward **intersection G12**. You've already hiked this section, albeit in the opposite direction, if you hiked the central loop described earlier. Going this way it's mostly a long descent.

At G12, turn right to follow the shore of Bull Sluice. The trail swings to the right as it turns up a small branch and begins to wind its way around a long and moderately narrow cove.

You'll eventually **ford the creek (29)** that forms the cove. It's a beautiful little creek, reminiscent of what you might see in the mountains of northern Georgia. And the setting is perfect, with the murmur of the brook and the whisper of wind the only sounds you hear.

The "lightning bolt tree" is one of many surprises awaiting you along the south loop trail.

Beyond the ford, the trail follows the cove back toward Bull Sluice and again follows the shoreline. For the next 500 yards or so the trail is pretty good, but you'll eventually encounter about 75 yards of rough and rocky going. Take your time as you pick your way over that more challenging section of trail.

A small wet-weather branch crosses the trail near the end of the rocky stretch, and about 150 yards beyond that you'll cross another small branch which rises from the deep gully to your right. A third such branch crosses the trail a few hundred yards farther on.

Beyond that third branch is a bit over 100 yards of fairly decent trail. But then the trail undergoes a sudden change of character, turning to red clay and beginning a **steep climb (30)** that continues for 150 yards or so.

After the climb, you'll enjoy about 40 paces of fairly level hiking before the trail begins to climb again. About 30 yards beyond the point where the climb starts, look for a short spur trail leading to the left. If you go a few yards down that trail and look to the left, you'll see the **"lightning bolt tree" (31)** – not a tree that's been hit by lightning, but instead a tree with a distinctive Z-shaped trunk shape which resembles a lightning bolt.

One explanation for the unusual trunk is some earlier event which caused the tree to be knocked out of vertical. Then when the tree tried to grow upwards, as trees naturally want to do, its trunk was shaped into the unusual form you see there now.

Back on the main trail, a bit more than 500 paces beyond the tree and near the point where the trail bends right, look left of the trail for a classic artifact of the southern woods: a

Several streams cross the Gold Branch Unit's trails, adding a perfect touch of ambience to these trails. Some crossings are on bridges. Others, as here, are less formal.

rusted piece of **bullet-riddled sheet metal (32)**. Exactly what it originally was is open to interpretation, but part of an old car is as good a guess as any.

The lightning bolt tree and the shot-up fender are just a few of the quirky surprises that await you along this section of trail. There are others...see if you can find 'em!

Another 500 or so yards of hiking along this trail takes you back to intersection G11. From there, turn left to backtrack to the trailhead – or turn right to hike the south loop trails again!

Morgan Falls Overlook Park

Morgan Falls Overlook Park, a City of Sandy Springs facility, is designed for family fun and features one of the neatest playgrounds I've ever seen. Your kids will love it. But the park offers hiking, too, with trails that provide great views of Bull Sluice Lake.

Bull Sluice Trail

From a **trailhead (1)** near a storage building at one corner of the parking area, the Bull Sluice Trail roughly parallels the edge of a portion of Bull Sluice, the lake formed by Morgan Falls Dam. Initially the trail follows along the side of the building; then, at the back of the building (at the end of a short boardwalk section) it turns left and soon traverses several timber steps. **Spur trails (2)** going uphill to the right take you out of the park, so stay on the main trail.

The trail soon turns right and passes a **swing (3)**. Beyond the swing you'll eventually **detour around a fallen tree (4)** and then **ford a small creek (5)** that flows from a spectacular rock outcrop a short distance upstream. More fallen trees (reminders of a severe storm that passed through the area in June 2013) obscure the view. Then come **more fallen trees (6)** – and just beyond them the trail ends near a large trailside **rock (7)**. At that point, turn around and return to the parking area.

The Overlook Trail

The second trail, and the only one shown on the park map posted near the playground, is the Overlook Trail – a looping trail that takes you up and along a ridge with great views of Bull Sluice. There are two trailheads, one at a corner of the parking area and one near a large pavilion beyond the playground. We'll start at the **parking area trailhead (8),** where three timber steps carry you up an incline and put you on the trail.

The trail passes through a fairly open area, then enters woods. You'll soon pass a **clearing (9)** on your left and a **bench (10)** on the right. This bench (like two similar benches further along the trail) was made from a felled cedar tree that once grew along the Overlook Trail route.

Beyond the bench is an **intersection (11)** with a connector trail which can shorten the hike if you wish. But to hike the whole loop, turn left at point 11. As you climb toward a ridge, notice evidence of terracing on the wooded slopes around you. You'll soon

Finding the trailhead

From GA 400: Take Exit 6 (Northridge Road) and go west for about a half mile to Roswell Road/GA 9. Turn left onto Roswell Road. Go 1.1 miles to Morgan Falls Road and turn right. Continue 1.3 miles to Morgan Falls Overlook Park on your right. To check out Morgan Falls Dam, continue 0.2 miles beyond the park to the dam's parking area.

This view from the Overlook Trails shows part of the park and of Bull Sluice – as well as the old stone chimney, all that remains of an early pioneer family's home which dates from the 1830s.

notice **downed trees (12)**, too, including some which as of this writing were laying across the trail. Getting past them is no problem, however. Beyond them another **wood bench (13)** offers a nice view, particularly during fall and winter. There's yet **another bench (14)** a bit further along.

Eventually you come to **several sets of timber steps (15)** that help you down a steep stretch. Beyond them is **intersection 16** with the other end of the cut-across connector. Go left to complete the final leg of the loop. Four more timber steps let you know that you're approaching the **second trailhead (17)**, which is located near a large covered pavilion.

Before calling it a day, check out the **stone chimney (18)** a short distance to your left. Dating from the 1830s, it was constructed using local fieldstone and is all that remains of an early pioneer family's home. The chimney was discovered in 2009 as the area was being cleared for construction of the park. Now it's a centerpiece of the park and a reminder of the area's rich history.

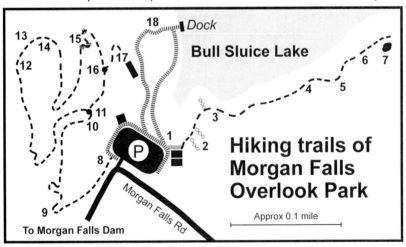

18 *Dock*

Bull Sluice Lake

13
14   15
12   16   17
6   7
4   5
11
10
3
1
P   2

8

9

To Morgan Falls Dam

Morgan Falls Rd

Hiking trails of Morgan Falls Overlook Park

Approx 0.1 mile

Johnson Ferry North

This mostly level trail provides easy hiking and a great chance of seeing wildlife.

During the nineteenth century, Johnson Garwood operated a ferry (the "Johnson" Ferry) near what's now Johnson Ferry Road. Fares were on a sliding scale that ranged from about 5 cents for an individual to a dollar or so for a loaded wagon plus its horse and driver. Today you cross the river for free on a modern highway bridge – and at the west end of the bridge, on the north side of the road, is CRNRA's Johnson Ferry North Unit.

This unit features a loop trail that traverses a forested wetland floodplain. The west leg follows the toe of a ridge (on your left) with wetlands on your right. The east leg closely parallels the river. Together, they make a great loop hike – and the entire loop is a great place for viewing a wide variety of wildlife.

Enter the unit through a **paved parking area** off Johnson Ferry Road just beyond the west end of the bridge. As you pull in, you'll see paved parking to your right and left. To the right (east), a **paved pedestrian path (1)** goes alongside the bridge and down toward the river. We'll say more about that in a moment.

Beyond the paved parking is a **graveled loop road** which leads to the **boat ramp (2)** and to **two buildings (3)** (restroom and covered picnic facilities) with other picnic tables nearby. Beyond the boat ramp is **a gravel parking area (4)** with pull-through spots designed for vehicles pulling boat trailers.

At the far end of the gravel parking area you'll find an **intersection (5)** with parallel paths that lead toward the loop trail. One is a two-track dirt road; the other is a utility right-of-way clearing which may be over-

Finding the trailhead

From I-285: Take Exit 24 (Riverside Drive) and go north for about 2.2 miles to Johnson Ferry Road. Turn left onto Johnson Ferry Road You'll soon cross the Chattahoochee. Immediately across the river, turn right into the Johnson Ferry North parking area.

grown. They're separated by a long, narrow band of undergrowth that's a favorite spot among bird watchers.

The path closest to the river, the two-track dirt road, leads to the actual **trailhead (6),** a gate-and-rock affair about 45 paces from the graveled loop road. The gate will probably be closed, and you'll find it easiest to go around it on the left.

Beyond the gate, the trail continues arrow-straight for about 250 yards, passing in and out of shade. It soon bends left and then right, intersecting the other end of the parallel trail. Just beyond the intersection is **Nannyberry Creek (7).**

Immediately beyond Nannyberry Creek you'll come to a **major trail intersection (8).** Continuing straight ahead takes you along the pipeline right-of-way. Turning right takes you to the river and upstream, carrying you around the loop in a counterclockwise direction. Turning left carries you around the loop clockwise. This guide goes clockwise, so turn left to begin exploring the loop.

Immediately after making the turn you'll see a sign identifying this as a great wildlife viewing area. To have the best chance of seeing wildlife here, the key is to be quiet and move slowly. Going early helps, and binoculars are a definite plus too.

Beyond the sign a **boardwalk (9)** crosses a wet area and a small creek. The boardwalk soon turns right, then yields to a dirt trail. At the end of the boardwalk a **spur (10)** goes left, but stay on the main trail.

About 70 paces beyond the boardwalk a **large fallen tree bridges the**

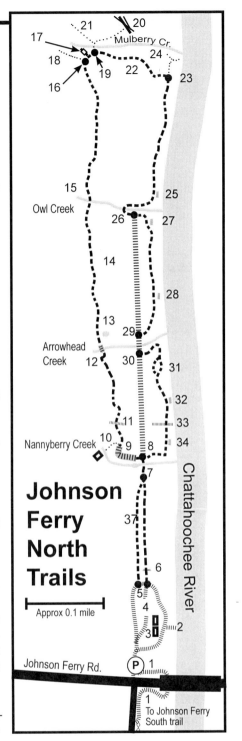

Johnson
Ferry
North
Trails

Approx 0.1 mile

Johnson Ferry Rd.

To Johnson Ferry
South trail

trail (11). If you're tall, you may need to duck.

Beyond the tree, the trail hugs the toe of the well-defined slope that rises off to your left. You'll traverse fairly level trail for about 250 yards, coming at last to a **short wooden bridge (12)** over Arrowhead Creek. But don't cross too quickly. Take time to check out the wetland habitat around the bridge.

I recently hiked this trail with son Nathan, who was home from college for the summer. As we came to the bridge, Nathan said, "Do you see that?"

I followed his gaze toward the edge of the creek, where a northern water snake rested almost invisibly among the leaves. The snake finally eased into gear and disappeared silently back into the undergrowth.

About 35 yards beyond the bridge a **large mound of dirt (13)** is visible to the right of the trail, and about 100 yards beyond it **wetlands (14)** appear to your right. It's incredible habitat for waterfowl, beavers, and other creatures that favor such environs. Several short spur trails lead to the right from the main trail and go down toward the wet area, providing excellent vantage points for observation or photography.

Here's how the gated trailhead will appear as you hike towards the main loop. Go around the gate on the left.

A couple of hundred yards of hiking brings you to a rocky area. Just beyond it you'll cross a **tiny branch and wet area (15)**, the beginning of Owl Creek.

The wet areas give way to woods, and you'll come to the **intersection (16)** that marks the northernmost point on the current version of this loop trail. This intersection is identified by a **map post (17)** which shows you where you are – but this spot also offers possibilities for confusion.

The first chance for confusion is a **spur trail (18)** to the left of the map post. It roughly parallels Mulberry Creek. A second spur turns left just past the map post, but it soon joins the first spur.

Yet another chance for confusion comes after you turn right at the map post. You'll come to an **intersection (19)** where you can turn right and follow Mulberry Creek toward the river – or you can go left and ford the creek.

The ford takes you to what was once a continuation of this hike. But that area is currently being restored. The trail beyond the creek only goes about 60 yards before a **large blown-down tree (20)** completely blocks the trail – and there are no obvious trails beyond it. You have to backtrack back to the main loop trail.

You may have noticed another small **spur trail (21)** on the far side of the creek. It too leads into an area that's currently closed. To avoid confusion don't cross the creek at all. Instead, continue southeast on the loop trail.

Going right (instead of fording the creek) leads you back toward the river. You'll pass a concrete sewer manhole on the left side of the trail. Soon after, the trail crosses the **pipeline right-of-way (22)**. You'll see a large pipe crossing the creek and signs indicating that the area across the creek is being reclaimed.

Continuing, you'll soon cross a small but distinctive ditch. About 85 yards beyond the ditch, you come to an **intersection (23)** where the main loop continues to the right and a **spur (24)** turns to the left. This spur takes you to the junction of Mulberry Creek with the Chattahoochee. It's about 75 yards to the junction, and along the way other short spur trails approach the river.

Back on the loop, follow the main trail back downriver. If you're hiking during the warmer months, you may notice that the cold water of the river serves as a sort of natural air conditioner along this leg of the hike.

Roughly 350 yards from the Mulberry Creek spur, you'll see a conveniently placed riverside **bench (25)** – the first of several such benches along this section of the trail. Beyond it, the trail swings to the right and goes away from the river to cross the **Owl Creek gully (26)**. Note the erosion control measures in this area. At that same point, the trail also intersects the far end of the pipeline clearing that you saw at the beginning of the loop.

To stay on the loop trail, go left toward the river once you cross the gully. The trail soon re-enters the woods and returns to the river. After a while there's **a second riverside bench (27)**. Another 140 or so paces brings you to **yet another bench (28)**. There's rest for the weary along this section of the trail!

Beyond the last bench, the trail again swings away from the river. Again, you're crossing a creek – Arrowhead Creek. The trail **intersects the pipeline clearing (29)** again. To your right, down the straight shot of the clearing, is the Owl Creek gully. To your left, down an equally straight shot, is the beginning of the loop. You may be able to hike back along the clearing, but it's much more scenic to re-enter the woods at **intersection 30** and follow the river trail.

The trail soon swings right and again begins to parallel the river, bringing you to an intersection where the **trail forks (31)**. Take either route; they rejoin just a few yards down the trail. The left part of the split runs *very* close to the water.

About 80 yards down the trail is **another bench (32)**. Beyond it you'll cross another, **smaller utility right of-way clearing (33)**. Just past it is a remarkably convenient **bench-shaped rock (34)** sitting to the left of the trail.

Beyond the bench rock the trail trends right, away from the river, and soon returns to the **intersection (8)** where you started the loop. From there, hike back toward the parking area. You can go left to backtrack along the trail you fol-

The Chattahoochee River will be your constant companion as you hike along the eastern leg of the Johnson Ferry North loop trail.

lowed coming in. Alternately, go right to parallel that trail and hike out along that long, straight clearing on the other side of the stretch of trees and brush. Either way it's a short walk back to your car.

And once you're back to your vehicle, is the hiking done? Maybe not! Remember that **paved pedestrian path (1)** that you noted at the beginning? Well, it takes hikers safely under the Johnson Ferry Road bridge (*much* safer than crossing the street itself) and then back to the intersection with Columns Drive.

From there, you can follow the sidewalk along Columns Drive until the sidewalk ends... then walk (carefully!) along the shoulder to the north end of the Johnson Ferry South trail, which is described next.

The Johnson Ferry North Unit trails provide outstanding opportunities for viewing wildlife. For best success, move quietly and watch carefully – and go early in the morning or late in the day.

Johnson Ferry South

The hiking trails of Johnson Ferry South offer an easy opportunity for a quick hike.

The trails of the Johnson Ferry South unit, while very close geographically to the Johnson Ferry North trail system, present you with an

The woods road trail at Johnson Ferry South is wide and level – a great place for a relaxing, low-effort stroll.

altogether different sort of hiking experience. One hiker has described these trails as "plain vanilla."

"They're not too exciting," she said. "They're flat and mostly straight."

But sometimes vanilla is what you want. Sometimes you want a quick and easy hike that lets you stretch your legs without having to think too hard. For those times the Johnson Ferry South trail may be just the trail for you.

As you might guess, the Johnson Ferry South unit of CRNRA is located south of Johnson Ferry Road. The **entrance (1)** is on Columns Drive off Johnson Ferry Road. Look for the **trailhead (2)** at a corner of the parking area. From there, the main trail goes left, following an **old woods road (3)**. About 200 paces beyond the trailhead, you'll cross a **small creek (4)**. A bit farther down the trail, there's another low and often **wet area (5)** about 500 paces beyond the creek. In between those two the trail provides good opportunities to look for wildlife in habitats ranging from fairly thick vegetation to relatively open woods.

Some of the terrain you'll pass through is identified as wetlands. It's no surprise that the area provides some potentially good wildlife viewing opportunities, and birders in particular will enjoy moving slowly along the trail (particularly during migration seasons) with binoculars at the ready.

The trail continues for approximately two-thirds of a mile. For most of that distance the woods road that you're following runs almost arrow-straight, paralleling the Chattahoochee River (which is off through the trees to your right) as well as Columns Drive (the road that you came in on). It is just about impos-

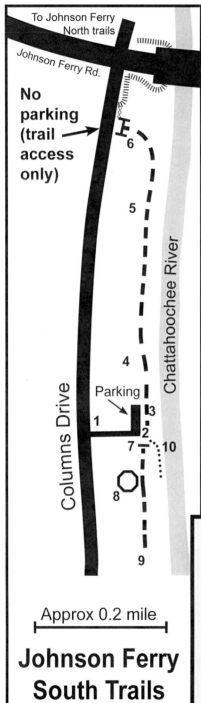

Johnson Ferry South Trails

Approx 0.2 mile

sible to lose your way.

As you approach the end of this trail, the woods will begin to give way to more grassy groundcover. The trail soon swings to the left, finally ending at a **second and gated access point (6)** (now closed to vehicles) at Columns Drive. From that point, simply turn around and backtrack the way you came to return to the main parking area and to your car.

Alternately, you can continue your hike into the Johnson Ferry North Unit and add that unit's great loop trail to your adventure. Cross under or around the gate (6), then turn right and follow the shoulder of Columns Drive to the start of a paved pedestrian sidewalk. Continue along the sidewalk to the intersection with Johnson Ferry Road. Then turn right. Turn right again where the pedestrian walkway swings off and begins to descend toward the river. It will pass under the Johnson Ferry Bridge (*much safer than crossing the road at the light*), then climb back up to the parking area for Johnson Ferry North as described in the previous section. Combining the two units' trails will give you the makings of a very enjoyable day of hiking.

Finding the trailhead

From I-285: Take Exit 24 (the Riverside Drive exit) and go north for approximately 2.3 miles to Johnson Ferry Road. Turn left on Johnson Ferry Road, and you'll cross the Chattahoochee river. After crossing the river, look for Columns Drive on your left. Make the left onto Columns Drive. Then go about 0.8 miles to the entry to the unit, which will be on your left.

The pavilion trail

Looking to the right from the main parking area, you'll see a large **gate (7)**; near it are some informational signs. If you turn right from the parking lot and go around the gate, instead of going left and following the woods road trail as just described, you'll find yourself in a large clearing that's the site of an **octagonal group shelter (8)**. The shelter is a great place to stop for a break, and its shade is especially welcome during the hotter months of the year.

Beyond the shelter and clearing, the woods close in again. The footpath continues in the clear for about 200 paces beyond the shelter, then **enters the woods (9)** and soon leaves park property.

Here's the view from the trailhead looking south (downstream). Note the large pavilion in the clearing a short distance from the parking area.

About that riverside spur trail...

While you were getting your bearings and preparing to explore the woods road and pavilion trails, you may have noticed a somewhat less well defined pathway heading off in the general direction of the river. It's an old **spur trail (10)**, a short, challenging, and in places very tightly overgrown path that, truth be told, is best left alone.

Exactly how long this spur trail is depends on your definition of "trail." For the first 100 paces it's fairly passable. But if you continue very far beyond that it quickly becomes overgrown – particularly in the summertime, when the predominant vegetation seems to be a combination of briars and an exceptionally healthy variety of poison ivy.

And be sure to note that it is also the home to a number of very low-hanging limbs and is one of the few places where I've literally and unexpectedly bonked my head while focusing my attention on the trail. That smarts! As if that wasn't enough, this trail seems to become even more rugged and uncertain the farther along it you go.

The bottom line? Although it beckons temptingly from the parking area trailhead, you'll be better off if you leave that riverside spur trail alone and enjoy much better riverside hiking elsewhere – either on one of the other Johnson Ferry South hiking routes or across Johnson Ferry Road on the Johnson Ferry North trails described in the previous section.

Sope Creek

Miles of hiking and ruins of a Civil War paper mill are just the beginning of what you'll find along the many and varied trails of Sope Creek.

There's a lot of history at Sope Creek. It's where an old covered bridge once crossed the creek...and where Federal forces first crossed the Chattahoochee River (just downstream at the mouth of Sope Creek) on July 8, 1864...and where the Marietta Paper Mills operated an extensive paper factory in the second half of the 19th century, producing (among other things) newsprint for many Georgia newspapers and (legend says) the paper used to print Confederate currency.

The extensive network of hiking trails in the Sope Creek Unit makes it easy to explore this area. Most hikes will begin at the parking area off Paper Mill Road, though it's also possible to start from other parking areas at Columns Drive or Cochran Shoals to the south.

With so many possibilities, how should you plan your Sope Creek hike? Every hiker will have his or her personal favorite routes. But one that almost everyone tackles sooner or later is the "big loop" – a trek around the unit's outer perimeter trails. It's an adventure that offers a taste of everything that Sope Creek has to offer...with a visit to the ruins of that old paper mill thrown in too!

When hiking at Sope Creek, note that sections of these trails are designated for hiking as well as biking. When on these shared trails, watch for bikes. Hikers have the right-of-way, but remember that on a twisting bike trail it can be hard for bikers to see hikers until they're right on top of each other. Common courtesy on the part of all concerned helps to make the shared-trail experience a good one.

And here's one final

Finding the trailhead

From I-285: From Interstate 285 take the Riverside Drive exit (exit 24) Go north on Riverside Drive for 2.3 miles to Johnson Ferry Road. Turn left on Johnson Ferry Road and go 2.7 miles to Paper Mill Road. Turn left onto Paper Mill Road and go 2.2 miles. The entrance to the Sope Creek Unit will be on the left after you cross Sope Creek.

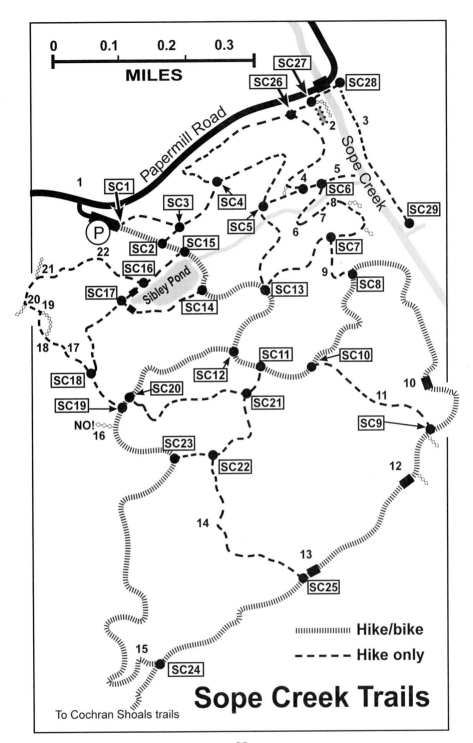

Sope Creek Trails

To Cochran Shoals trails

|||||||||| Hike/bike
- - - - - Hike only

The Sope Creek trailhead. The hike/bike trail begins behind the gate; to the left, a hiking-only trail begins.

note: The National Park Service intersection identifiers referred to in this chapter are those currently used on these trails. Some older maps show different intersection numbers that are no longer accurate, but the ones used here are current.

Hiking the loop

The **entrance (1)** to the Sope Creek unit is off Paper Mill Road. The trails begin at intersection **SC1** at the far end of the parking area behind a group of signs. Actually, two trails begin there – a road-like gravel trail that starts behind a gate (the shared trail for hikers and bikers) and a dirt trail to the left of the signs. To begin this loop, follow the dirt trail to the left toward **intersection SC3**. Then, at SC3, turn left along a gently descending trail toward **intersection SC4**.

At SC4, go left. The trail descends for about 130 paces to a hairpin turn to

the right, then continues downhill parallel to Paper Mill Road. A small creek flows down the hill below you. You'll find some rough sections of trail as you go.

You'll soon reach an intersection **(SC26).** Just beyond it the trail swings down toward the road, and then there they are beyond **intersection SC27**: the **ruins of the old Marietta Paper Mills (2)**. You'll see **additional ruins (3)** across the creek. The mill complex manufactured a variety of paper products, including newsprint and stationery and

Sope Creek as seen from near the old Marietta Paper Mills ruins.

86

(some say) the paper used to print Confederate currency. The site was burned July 5, 1864, by Federal forces. After the war it was rebuilt, only to burn again in 1870. Rebuilt yet again, it operated until 1902. Historic markers near the parking area tell the story in detail.

Several trails meander among the ruins, allowing you to explore them thoroughly. There are more ruins on the other side of the creek, and another trail goes down that far side starting at a point across the bridge **(SC28)**.

After exploring the ruins, return to the loop trail route at **SC26** and go left toward **point 4,** an intersection with a wide trail. You'll see a short spur going to the right just before point 4, but stay on the main trail.

At point 4, turn left on the wide trail. You'll soon come to **intersection SC6.** Go right at SC6 to continue the loop, but first take a moment to walk down the **spur (5)** for some very nice views of Sope Creek.

From SC6, hike toward SC7. The trail descends and crosses a tiny branch, then follows a bigger branch upstream to a **hairpin bend (6)** to the left. You'll ford the creek at the hairpin, and there's a great sitting rock just beyond the ford.

Beyond the rock the trail climbs moderately for about 90 paces, then levels off. You'll see some **stacked stone walls (7)** along the uphill side of the trail. About 80 paces beyond them, a **"lightning bolt" tree (8)** grows in the middle of the trail. The Z-shaped trunk of the tree testifies to something which happened in the past and caused the trunk to grow in that configuration.

Mountain biking enthusiast Hank Smith crosses one of the bridges on the hike/bike portion of the Sope Creek loop.

Beyond the lightning-bolt tree, a rough spur trail goes left. A second spur is evident about 100 paces further on. The main trail, however, continues to **intersection SC7.**

Going right at SC7 would take you off the loop and put you on a long stretch of trail which follows a ridge to **intersection SC13** and the main hike/bike trail. To continue the loop, however, go left at SC7 toward **SC8,** another intersection with the hike/bike trail.

The trail from SC7 to SC8 starts out level but then **descends fairly sharply**

(9) to a ford over a small creek. The SC8 intersection is just beyond the ford. SC8 is an intersection with the combined hike/bike trail, which you'll now follow for quite a ways. As noted earlier, mutual courtesy between hikers and bikers is the key to happy times on a trail such as this. And with that sage advice in mind, turn left at SC8 to continue the loop.

The trail between SC8 and SC9, the next intersection, is scenic. For much of the way you'll hear (and may see) Sope Creek flowing in the gorge below you. Just don't get so wrapped up in the scene that you forget to watch for bikes!

You'll soon come to a **bridge (10)** in a hairpin turn. Not far beyond it is **intersection SC9.** There, you could turn right past a "no bikes" sign and hike a foot-traffic-only trail toward **intersection SC10** with the hike/bike trail. Or you can stay on the main trail to continue the loop, which soon brings you to another **bridge (12).** Between bridges 10 and 12, several spurs go left. Ignore them.

Some distance down the trail is yet **another bridge (13)** and, just beyond it, **intersection SC25.** At SC25, a right turn puts you on another cut-across trail that leads to SC22, SC21 and eventually back to the hike/bike trail at SC11. This trail climbs fairly steeply as you start up it from SC25. Further along, it **fords a tiny creek (14)** and soon comes to intersections (SC22 and SC21) with other connecting trails leading to SC23 and SC20.

The loop, however, continues straight at SC25. From SC25 it's easy hiking to **intersection SC24,** where a left takes you to the trails of Cochran Shoals (covered separately). The current loop hike goes right at SC24 and soon **fords a small creek (15).** Beyond the ford is good trail with some long ascents and descents as you move toward **intersection SC23.**

At SC23 a connector goes right toward SC22, but the loop hike (still on hike/bike trail) goes straight. You'll soon come to an intersection with a spur trail **(16)** which goes left, but that spur takes you toward the edge of CRNRA property. So continue on the main trail for about 50 more yards to **intersection SC19** – and that's where things get a little tricky.

SC19 to SC16: Navigating the tricky section

The trails of Sope Creek are generally well marked. In fact, only one group of trails – those west of Sibley Pond – is potentially confusing.

What's the reason for the confusion? Numerous "social trails" branch from the designated route in this area, and some create the real possibility of confusion. Thus, here's how to navigate that section as part of our clockwise hike around the main loop – without getting lost.

At **intersection SC19,** leave the hike/bike trail and continue the loop by turning left and hiking about 200 paces on a foot-traffic-only trail to **intersection SC18.** Turning right at SC18 takes you along a creek gully toward Sibley Pond, bypassing the tricky section. But continue straight at SC18 to stay on the loop.

About 45 paces beyond the intersection, the trail leaves the woods and enters an overgrown **clearing (17).** You'll follow a clearly defined path, ascending for about 180 paces to the hill's crest and **point 18,** where a lightly-used spur trail (it may be overgrown) turns right while the main trail goes straight and down the hill. The spur and main trail soon come back together at **point 19.**

If you've stayed on the main trail and not taken the spur, turn left at **intersection 19.** Then hike about 65 paces to an **intersection (20)** with a cross trail. Turning left would put you on a spur that winds off into the woods, but don't take that spur. Instead, **turn right at point 20** to stay on the loop.

About 15 paces after the turn, you'll pass through an old cut log, and about ten paces beyond that log the trail bends distinctly to the right.

Then, roughly 64 paces beyond the cut log (that is, about 80 paces beyond the intersection at **point 20,** you'll see a spur trail going left at **point 21.** Don't take the spur but stay to the right to remain on the main trail.

Beyond that intersection, the trail continues without confusion for about 280 paces to a **section of fence (22)** marking a closed area. Then, about 180 paces beyond the fence, you'll come to **intersection SC16** near the upper end of the lake. You've made it!

Finishing the loop

From SC16 it's smooth sailing back to the parking area. The direct route is to turn left at SC16 and hike along the lake to **intersection SC15** with the hike/bike trail. Turn left at that point and follow the wide trail up the hill through **intersection SC2** and back to the parking area, completing the Sope Creek loop.

The Sibley Pond loop hike

The loop trail hike described in this chapter gives you plenty of material for an enjoyable day of hiking, especially when combined with various connector trails. But if you don't have a lot of time, one enjoyable Sope Creek excursion is a much  shorter loop hike around the lake. From the **parking lot,** follow the hike/bike trail through **intersection SC2** to **intersection SC15,** near one end of the Sibley Pond dam. From that point you can hike the lake loop in either direction. This loop hike is a particularly good one to enjoy with young children.

Cochran Shoals

From wetlands to ridges, you'll find it all on the trails of Cochran Shoals.

Cochran Shoals is one of the most visited CRNRA units, and if you're a hiker's it's easy to see why. It offers an incredible array of trails – everything from intimate wooded paths and a boardwalk through wetlands to hikes beside streams, walks along ridges, and everything in between. You'll find hiking-only as well as hike/bike trails. There's even a three-mile graveled fitness loop trail, perfect for folks who like their hiking less wild and more urban.

Two parking areas provide access. One, at the end of Columns Drive (point **CS10**), provides convenient access to unit's northern trails. The second, off Interstate North Parkway (point **CS35**), provides easy access to the "Interstate North" set of trails in the southern portion of the unit. Either access point provides direct access to the fitness trail. Because this area is so popular, these parking areas may fill up on weekends or weekday afternoons, with cars waiting for a space to open up.

We'll look first at the fitness trail, then at the north-end hike and hike/bike trails, and finally at the Interstate North group of trails at the unit's southern end.

The fitness trail

One reason for this unit's popularity is the Cochran Shoals fitness trail. This wide and level gravel trail is popular

---

Finding the trailheads

Columns Drive trailhead from I-285:
Take Exit 24 (Riverside Drive) and go north for about 2.2 miles to Johnson Ferry Road. Turn left onto Johnson Ferry Road. You'll soon cross the Chattahoochee. Immediately across the river, turn left onto Columns drive. Follow Columns Drive for roughly 2.6 miles; Columns Drive will end at the Columns Drive parking area.

Interstate North Parkway trailhead from I-285: Take exit 22 (Northside Drive, New Northside Drive, Powers Ferry Road) and go to Interstate North Parkway. The parking area is on the right off Interstate North Parkway just west of

Cochran Shoals trail highlights include a wetlands boardwalk (left) and a wide, level and graveled multi-use fitness trail (right).

with joggers, walkers, bikers, and even parents pushing strollers. Aside from being very enjoyable by itself, it's also a gateway to other Cochran Shoals hiking opportunities.

The fitness trail is accessible from either of the unit's parking areas and includes a loop that can be hiked in either direction.

This guide starts at the Interstate North Parkway trailhead **(CS35)**. Hiking upriver from that point, you'll see picnic tables on your left. Behind them rises a rocky bluff – and in that bluff are overhanging **rock shelters (17)**, accessible via a short spur. Such overhangs provided shelter for the area's earliest inhabitants, and you'll find similar shelters at several locations within CRNRA.

Not far past the rock shelters a **dirt side trail (18)** branches right and parallels the fitness trail for a short distance. It rejoins the graveled path at the 0.25 mile marker. Beyond that point you'll cross a **concrete bridge (19)** and then

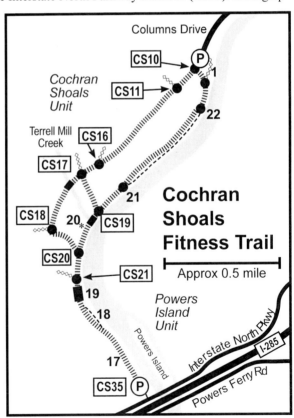

Gators on the Hooch?

There was talk at one time about alligator sightings at Cochran Shoals. Are there really gators in the Chattahoochee?

As it turns out, there may have been at least one. Occasional sightings since 2007 have reported a gator in the 6 to 8 foot range. Some said it was even bigger!

Alligators don't naturally live this far north, so how could one end up in Atlanta's Chattahoochee? It was probably a pet that was released when it got too big to keep.

According to the National Park Service, alligators "tend to exhibit a natural fear of humans and do not pose a threat unless provoked." In other words, if by any chance you happen to see one, just leave it alone.

come to **intersection CS21,** where a dirt trail goes left toward the Interstate North group of trails.

Continue the fitness trail by hiking toward **intersection CS20,** the beginning of the loop part of the fitness trail. We'll go counterclockwise around the loop portion, so hike straight on. Look for a **water fountain (20)** on the left. Beyond it is a bridge over Terrell Mill Creek, and just beyond that is an intersection **(CS19)** with a cut-across trail which connects with the far side of the loop.

You'll soon see a dirt trail forking right **(21)** to parallel the graveled trail for about a half mile. It fords a small creek, then rejoins the main route at **point 22.**

Beyond point 22, the fitness trail curves left. A **spur (1)** goes right toward a gate near the parking area, but the main trail, continues to **intersection CS10** and the northern fitness trail trailhead at the end of Columns Drive.

To continue the fitness trail loop, turn left at CS10 and hike toward **intersection CS11,** one of the access points for the north-end hiking trails. Beyond it are **intersections CS16** and **CS17,** additional access points to the north-end trails. At CS17 you can go straight or turn left toward the river (that is, toward CS19) on that cut-across trail through the wetlands area.

If you go straight, the trail again crosses Terrell Mill Creek. It then comes to **intersection CS18,** an access point to the Interstate North trails. From that point, if you look ahead along the right-of-way clearing that stretches away into the distance, you may spot one of the Interstate North trails as it follows the right-of-way up the side of a ridge.

Just beyond CS18 the fitness trail swings left toward intersection CS20. Turn right at CS20 to return to the Interstate North parking area.

North-end loop hike from Columns Drive parking area

Cochran Shoals' north-end hike/bike trails make for a great loop hike that carries you across some remarkably scenic terrain. Starting at the parking area at the end of Columns Drive, look for the intersection with the fitness trail (**CS10**) behind a gate at the back right corner of the parking lot. Then follow the fitness trail to **intersection CS11.** There, turn right onto a hike-only trail that climbs about 100 yards to **intersection CS12** with the hike/bike trail. That's where this loop hike begins.

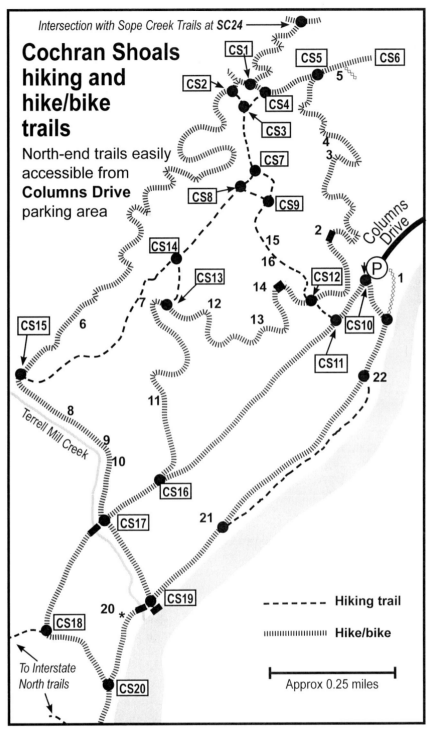

Intersection with Sope Creek Trails at **SC24** →

Cochran Shoals hiking and hike/bike trails

North-end trails easily accessible from **Columns Drive** parking area

CS1
CS5   CS6
CS2   CS4
CS3
5
CS7   4
CS8   3
CS9
2
15
16
CS14
CS13   CS12
14   1
7   12   CS10
13
CS11
CS15   6
22
11
Terrell Mill Creek
8
9
10
CS16
21
CS17
CS19
20 *
CS18
To Interstate North trails
CS20

- - - - - - - **Hiking trail**

||||||||||||||||| **Hike/bike**

Approx 0.25 miles

Columns Drive

P

When hiking this loop, remember that you're hiking on a trail that's shared by hikers and bikers. As noted elsewhere, the key to making shared trails work is simple courtesy among all concerned. I've had only good experiences on these trails, and I've found the mountain bikers I've met to be courteous and careful. Yes, there may be bad apples in any batch (and that includes hikers as well as bikers). But remember "do unto others" and you'll be doing your part to ensure an enjoyable outdoor experience for all – hikers and bikers alike.

To explore the loop, start by turning right at **CS12**. The trail descends and eventually fords a small creek; beyond the ford is a small **bridge (2)** over another creek – and then a *long* climb to **intersection CS5**. Along the way you'll pass two fence sections **(points 3 and 4)** which mark areas that have been closed to allow restoration. You'll see several such fence sections on these trails.

Deer are very common along CRNRA's trails, and you're likely to spot them at almost any time.

At **CS5,** turning right takes you along a pleasant trail and past a **spur trail (5)** going right. About 180 paces beyond the spur is the park boundary at **CS6**. But to continue the loop, go *left* from CS5 for about 200 yards to **intersection CS4** – and then go right from CS4 toward **intersection CS1.**

At CS1 a right turn puts you on the connector leading to the Sope Creek trail system. The connector descends for several hundred yards, crossing a bridge over a creek and then fording a second stream before ascending to **intersection SC24** and the south end of the Sope Creek trails.

To stay on the present loop, however, go straight at CS1 to **intersection CS2**. You'll see a trail turning right (it quickly leaves park property) while the main trail trends left. Just a few yards further, a dirt hiking-only trail turns left behind "no bikes" signs, while the main bike/hike trail swings right. This spread-out intersection sounds confusing, but it makes sense when you see it on the ground.

The main hike/bike trail now begins a long run that continues to **intersection CS15**. It's a particularly scenic stretch, and it goes on for a long time – almost 2,600 paces, according to a recent count. Yes, I really counted!

Volunteers help keep this and other CRNRA trails clear, but it's always possible that you may encounter a newly fallen tree. That happened to me recently when I found a formerly clear section of trail blocked by a just-fallen tree (it happened at **point 6**). The top of the tree had landed on the trail, and the resulting tangle of smashed limbs completely obscured several yards of what was otherwise an easy-to-follow path. There was no alternative but to pick my way through and around the tangle, finally regaining clear trail on the other side.

A little while later I shared my downed-tree discovery with a mountain biker who was coming up the trail from the other direction.

"A new tree down?" he said, shaking his head. "We just cleared that trail!" When you finally reach CS15 you've descended the ridge to Terrell Mill Creek. At CS15 a fairly rough trail goes off to your left and uphill. That's one end of a hiking-only trail that leads to **intersection CS14.** More on it later. For now, stay on the loop and take the trail that closely follows the creek downstream. Initially it's rough and rocky. But once you get past the rocky stretch and can pay attention to something besides your footing, be sure to notice the creek. It's a beautiful stream with splashing cascades and noisy riffles that provide a perfect soundtrack for hiking.

Note that you may encounter a **significant muddy stretch (8)** about half way to CS17. Smaller **muddy patches (9 and 10)** may await you further along too.

The creekside trail eventually intersects the fitness trail at **intersection CS17.** Turn left there and follow the fitness trail to **intersection CS16,** where a left turn takes you back into the woods to continue the loop (still on hike/bike trail).

A series of widely spaced wood timbers set across the trail greets you as you begin the ascent from CS16. You'll eventually come to a **fence section (11)** marking a closed area. Soon thereafter the trail bends right, then swings broadly left and climbs toward another sharp bend to the right – and just past *that* bend is **intersection CS13** with a hike-only trail that climbs to **intersection CS14.** The hike/bike loop, however, begins a descent toward **intersection CS12.**

Between CS13 and CS12 you'll ford a couple of small streams **(points 12 and 13)** and eventually cross a larger stream on a **small bridge (14).** About 200 paces beyond that bridge is **intersection C12** where you began the loop.

Hiking the interior

What about those intriguing hiking-only trails in the interior of this portion of the Cochran Shoals Unit? These north-end interior trails make it easy to plan a long ridge hike that can be incorporated into your Cochran Shoals hiking in many ways. Here's one interesting possibility that includes not only the hiking-only trails but also some sections of the unit's hike/bike trails.

Start at the **main trailhead (CS10)** at the Columns Drive parking area; then hike through **CS11** and **CS16** to **CS17.** Turn right at CS17 and follow the hike/bike trail up Terrell Mill Creek to **intersection CS15.** But instead of making a 90-degree turn to follow the hike/bike trail, make a *sharp* right onto that rough and (at first) steep and rocky hiking-only trail. Fortunately, the tough stretch lasts for only 100 yards or so, and things moderate as you climb up onto the ridge.

You'll eventually pass a **fence section (7)** marking a closed-for-restoration area; beyond it is relatively smooth sailing to **intersection CS14.** At CS14 you could turn right and descend along a short connector to pick up the hike/bike trail at CS13...or you could continue along the ridge toward **intersection CS8.**

The trails connecting **CS7, CS8** and **CS9** form a sort of roundabout that lets you jump off in various directions. For example, you can make the hike from CS8 to CS7, then swing left toward CS2 or CS4 on the main hike/bike trail.

In any case, be sure to note the small **Scribner family cemetery** at CS9. This cemetery, which has been restored, is one of several tiny family cemeteries scattered through the area. It includes graves from the 19th century.

From CS9 the most direct way back to the trailhead is via the long descent to CS12 and then to CS11. Along the way you'll encounter a series of six widely spaced stacked stone steps; beyond the last one is what hikers have come to call the **"tunnel tree" (16)** on the right side of the trail. This tree has a hollow trunk which, at ground level, forms a tiny natural bridge. See if you can spot it!

Not far beyond the tunnel tree the trail levels a bit, then descends again, then comes at last to **intersection CS12**. From there you can continue straight ahead to **intersection CS11** and the graveled fitness trail.

The "Interstate North" trails from Interstate North parking area

There's more great Cochran Shoals hiking awaiting you along the so-called

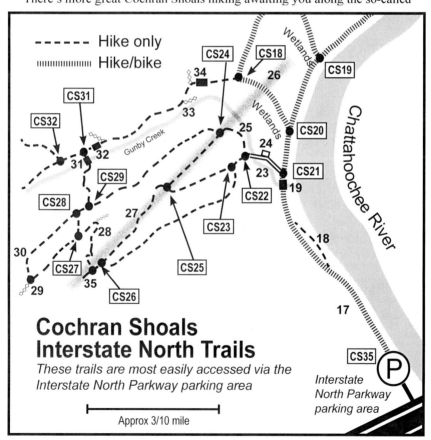

Cochran Shoals
Interstate North Trails

These trails are most easily accessed via the Interstate North Parkway parking area

Approx 3/10 mile

Interstate
North Parkway
parking area

"Interstate North" trails, a group of hiking-only pathways near the south end of the unit. They're best accessed from the parking area off Interstate North Parkway – thus their name. On a map, this appears to be a small and densely packed group of trails. It is indeed compact. But there's a *lot* of trail packed into that small area – and some of it is challenging trail too.

Begin at the **Interstate North Parkway trailhead (CS35)** and hike up the river along the graveled fitness trail to **intersection CS21**. Turn left at that point, and a few more steps will put you a long **boardwalk (23)** that winds its way across a wetlands area. There's an **observation platform (24)** partway along the boardwalk. Birders enjoy this part of the Cochran Shoals Unit, which offers excellent birding opportunities for binocular-equipped hikers.

The boardwalk meanders through the swampy area for more than 200 yards, ending at last at an **intersection (CS22)** where you can go right or continue straight ahead.

And that's where the hiking here can get complicated.

Here's the view from intersection CS24 looking northeast. The curving trail in the background is part of the Cochran Shoals fitness trail.

From that point on, these trails form a weblike network that offers myriad routings. It's a question of which way to go, and there are a lot of possible answers. Here are some trail notes that may help you decide which paths to take.

CS22 to CS24: Hiked from CS22 to CS24, this trail may start off wet (if it's rained recently) but then climbs a bit and dries out. Look for a **large fallen tree (25)** on the right; just beyond it is a relatively steep climb up to a **gas line right-of-way (26)**. As you enter the right-of-way, ignore the faint spur that goes straight ahead. Instead, go left for a few yards to intersection CS24.

CS24 to CS25: This section of trail follows a narrow but well-defined path along the gas line right-of-way, eventually dead-ending in a cross trail at CS25.

CS25 to CS26: Here's another section that follows the gas line right-of-way. However, this one's more challenging. Coming from CS25, you'll have a steep climb up toward CS26, including **one very steep and rocky stretch (27)** that calls for careful attention to your footing.

CS26 to CS23: From CS26, a trail turns left and enters the woods; it's bound for CS23. This is a very scenic trail. Hiked in this direction, it first follows the ridge and then begins a steady descent that's steep and rooty in places – especially over the last few yards approaching CS23.

CS26 to CS27: A few yards beyond CS26, at an info board and a "no bikes" sign, a trail turns right at **point 35** and cuts across the right-of-way clearing bound for CS27. Watch your footing as you re-enter the woods on the far side of the clearing (near another "no bikes" sign). Once in the woods, you're in for a steep and rough descent to a **ford (28)** over a creek. Beyond it, the trail makes a hairpin turn to the left and begins to climb a rough stretch. Be sure to make that left turn; don't be distracted by the spur.

CS27 to CS28 via cut-across trail: Hiked in this direction, this is a steady climb of about 150 yards.

CS27 to CS28 via loop: This route takes you to the very edge of park property. The first leg (CS27 to point 29) is level and ends very close to a large building. Turn right and hike uphill (essentially along the park boundary) to point 30; then go right to CS28.

CS28 to CS29: A short, easy connector.

CS29 to CS24: Starting at CS29, the trail challenges you for a hundred yards or so with two rocky stretches through relatively narrow cuts. Beyond them, it's pleasant hiking to the gas line clearing and CS24.

CS29 to CS31: Here's a steady descent that's complicated in many areas by rocks and roots. Use caution. At the bottom, a **bridge (31)** crosses a very picturesque creek just before CS31.

CS31 to CS32: This section follows a level utility clearing.

Beyond CS32: The trail (actually, the utility right-of-way clearing) forks at CS32. The right fork climbs a hill, fords a creek, and then dead-ends at private property. The left fork goes straight, fords two creeks, and then curves sharply right before dead-ending at a road.

CS31 to CS18: Hiking from CS31 toward CS18, you'll immediately cross another **wood footbridge (32)**. Beyond the bridge the trail follows the creek for some distance, but you'll then find the creekside route becomes muddy and **ends (33)**. Before the muddy patch, a bypass trail swings left. Take the bypass, trending right at intersections with social trails (there are many in this area). You're looking for a **wood footbridge (34)**. This area is confusing because of the large number of social trails, but the wood footbridge is the key.

Once across that bridge, ignore spurs leading left and stay on the main trail, which skirts wetlands on its right before emerging from the woods to rejoin the fitness trail at intersection CS18.

Powers Island

Much less heavily used than Cochran Shoals across the river, the Powers Island Unit packs a lot of hiking variety into a small area.

The bridge to Powers Island as it appears when you're looking toward the island.

On your way to the Powers Island Unit, you may have crossed the river on a modern highway bridge. But in the early nineteenth century, the way to cross was via ferry. Plantation owner James Powers took advantage of that to build and operate a ferry here, and that's how Powers Island got its name.

The Powers Island trail network offers a variety of hiking opportunities that range from flat floodplain walks to strenuous (but very scenic) hikes up and down ridges. In fact, there are three distinctly different hikes at Powers Island. One is the island hike, a loop hike located on the island itself. The second hike, the floodplain hike, is a long loop that takes you upriver (on the mainland) from the parking area. At the top of that loop, an in-and-out trail continues upriver to the park boundary. Each of these hikes is essentially level. But the third hike, by far the most challenging of the three, is a loop that goes up and down along ridges – carrying you out along one ridge and back along another – with leg-stretching climbs and descents along the way.

All Powers Island hikes begin at the unit's parking area just off Interstate North Parkway. There are actually three trailheads. The floodplain and ridge hikes begin and end at one of two trailheads at the far end of the parking area, while the Powers Island hike begins at a paved trailhead near the concession building on the Interstate North Parkway end of the parking area.

The Powers Island Hike

Powers Island, for which this unit is named, offers hikers a nice half-mile loop that traverses the northern portion of the island. The trailhead is located

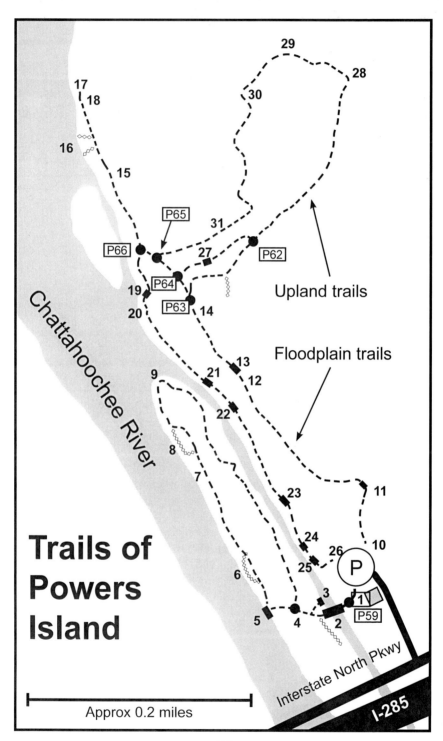

Trails of Powers Island

Chattahoochee River

Upland trails

Floodplain trails

P65
P66
P64
P63
P62
P59

Approx 0.2 miles

Interstate North Pkwy

I-285

at the south end of the main parking area near the concession building, where a **short paved approach (1)** leads from the parking area to a **bridge (2)** which spans the channel between Powers Island and the mainland.

Just beyond the bridge, an overgrown spur trail goes left. But stay on the main trail, which is wide and graveled. You'll see **concrete steps leading down to the water (3)** on your right. Beyond them, the trail continues across the island, passing an **intersection (4)** and continuing on to the **primary boat and raft launch (5)** on the island's far (river) side. Near the launch area are several benches as well as an informational plaque describing how the group known as the "River Rats," along with the Georgia Conservancy, the Georgia Wildlife Federation and interested citizens, formed "Friends of the River" in 1971. That group pushed for and helped gain protection for this area, working with the Department of the Interior to develop a plan for a national recreation area along a 48-mile stretch of the Chattahoochee. That's how the Chattahoochee River National Recreation Area came to be born.

The loop trail begins at the launching area, where a clear trail heads off upriver. About 30 paces brings you to an intersection with a **spur trail (6)** that goes left; the spur soon rejoins the main trail.

Roughly 200 yards further, the trail passes over a **cut log (7)** that's been notched to allow easy passage. Beyond it is an intersection with another **spur trail (8)** that goes off to the left but also soon rejoins the main loop.

Finding the trailhead

From eastbound I-285: Take exit 22 (Northside Drive, New Northside Drive, Powers Ferry Road). Go straight to the second traffic light and turn left onto New Northside Drive. Pick up the "through" lane to Interstate North Parkway. Continue about 0.6 miles to the entrance, which will be on the right just before you cross the river.

From westbound I-285: Take exit 22 (Northside Drive, New Northside Drive, Powers Ferry Road) and turn right on New Northside Drive. Continue onto Interstate North Parkway. Continue for about 0.6 miles to the entrance, which will be on the right just before you cross the river.

You're now nearing the upstream end of Powers Island. At that point, the trail makes a **sharp right (9)**, then swings away from the main river as it cuts across the island and begins its return leg. The path meanders on its way to the **intersection (4)** with the main gravel trail leading from the bridge to the primary boat and raft launch.

The floodplain hike

The island loop is a good warm-up for the longer, but still easy, floodplain loop hike. From the parking area, this hike begins with one leg of the loop (we'll go counterclockwise), then does an out-and-back hike which takes you to the park boundary, and then returns to the parking area on the other leg of the loop.

Start at the **trailhead (10)** at the back corner of the parking area (near a fee kiosk and a gate) and follow a wide, graveled path that curves right before swinging left to cross a small **creek (11)**. Beyond the creek the trail follows the inland edge of the floodplain. After about 300 yards, look for a **tree growing atop a large rock (12)** on the right side of the trail; about 40 paces beyond it you'll cross **another creek (13)** that passes through a pipe under the trail. At this point, you're nearing the upper end of Powers Island.

Another 80 or so yards brings you to a point where the trail passes between two timbers that have been laid almost flush with the ground. Then, about 70 yards further, look for **rock formations (14)** to the right of the trail. The area's earliest inhabitants used such overhangs for shelter, and you'll see more of them elsewhere in CRNRA...even further along on this particular hike.

Continuing, you'll soon come to **intersection P63**, the first of three intersections that you can use to access the ridge loop hike (covered separately). The others are **P64** and **P65**. For now, however, continue straight on the main trail.

Just beyond P65 is **intersection P66,** where you go straight to hike the "in" part of the in-and-out portion of this hike...or you can go left and downstream to complete the loop part of the hike.

Hiker John Miller and daughter Adaline, age 6 months, get ready to hike the trails of Powers Island. It's never too early to introduce a young person to hiking!

To continue the in-and-out hike, go upstream at P66 beside a channel between a small island and the mainland. As you near the upper end of that island, look right for **more overhanging rock ledges (15)**. Not far beyond them you'll see **two short spurs (16)** going left toward the river, and not far beyond those spurs is a **prominent no-trespassing sign (17)** that reads "LEAVING NATIONAL FOREST Private Property NO TRESPASSING." Although there's trail beyond that sign, the message is clear. Turn around and backtrack toward intersection P66 – but not before checking out one last sheltering **rock overhang (18)** located just off the trail a few yards before you get to the sign.

To complete the loop on your return hike, take the right fork at P66 and hike downstream. You'll cross a small **bridge (19)**, the first of several on this leg of the loop. Just beyond it you'll detour to the left around a **large fallen tree (20)**. Past the detour, the upper end of Powers Island soon comes into view. Beyond it you'll cross **five small foot bridges (21, 22, 23, 24, 25)**. Just past the last of those bridges, the trail makes a sharp left, passes between two large rocks, and ends at a **trailhead (26)** at a corner of the main parking area across from where you started.

The ridge loop

Okay...you've done the easy trails. Now it's time for the ridge loop.

The ridge loop, accessible from the upper end of the loop portion of the floodplain hike, starts off easy but then challenges you with long and occasionally steep ascents and descents. It is a scenic

A lone jogger enjoys a run on the in-and-out portion of the floodplain trail.

trail, and in the spring the wildflowers can be spectacular. You can hike this loop in either direction; this guide will go counterclockwise.

Start by hiking to **intersection P63,** where a right turn puts you on the loop. You'll immediately begin to climb. As you go, watch out for old metal pipes crossing the trail. Some of those old pipes are torn and have jagged edges exposed.

About 130 paces into your climb you may notice a spur trail going off to the right, but stay on the main trail. The main trail soon brings you to **intersection P62,** an intersection with a second access trail (the one which starts at **intersection P64).** That too is a very scenic trail; it includes a **bridge (27)** over a tiny creek, some interesting stonework just beyond the bridge, and steps (timber in one place, stone in another) to help you over a couple of steep spots.

Beyond P62 the trail levels for just a little while but then begins a very long climb. It eventually swings left as it approaches a high spot, then climbs very gently along a ridge before beginning at last to descend at **point 29.**

The trail has one more very short but rigorous **climb (30)** in store, but then it's a long and steady downhill back toward the floodplain loop. To your right is high ground; to your left, below you, flows a tiny creek.

Eventually you'll come to a set of **five widely-space timber steps (31)** which helps you to negotiate a steep section of the trail. Not far beyond, at another steep stretch, is a second set of similar but much more weathered steps

Beyond the steps, the descent becomes increasingly gentle as the pathway approaches the floodplain trail and the end of the ridge loop at **intersection P65.** From there, turn left to return to the main trailhead or right to continue upriver.

Paces Mill and Sandy Point

A jogger enjoys a morning outing along the Rottenwood Creek Trail.

Near the spot where I-285 and I-75 meet, the trails of Paces Mill and Sandy Point/Palisades West offer great hiking (sometimes within sight of the interstate) and a perfect alternative to sitting in rush hour traffic.

The Paces Mill area offers miles of great hiking over diverse and very scenic terrain. CRNRA provides two access points for these trails. On the south end is the Paces Mill parking area off Cobb Parkway/US-41. The second access, to the north, is via Sandy Point/Palisades West parking area accessible from Akers Mill Road. It provides access to the "Sandy Point" area, popular with hikers and kayakers alike.

The're also a third access point outside CRNRA at the trailhead for the Bob Callan Trail, a paved trail connecting with a similar trail originating at the Paces Mill parking area. There's a *tiny* parking area at the Bob Callan trailhead, but it's often full.

We'll look at four different hikes in this area: the Rottenwood Creek/Bob Callan Trail hike, the central loop hike, the Sandy Point connector, and the Sandy Point trails.

> ## Finding the trailheads:
>
> The Paces Mill trailhead is off Cobb Parkway/US-41 just north of the bridge carrying that road over the river. Simply exit I-285 at Cobb Parkway/US-41 and head south for about 1.4 miles to the Paces Mill parking area, just before crossing the river.
>
> To reach the Akers Drive trailhead, take Akers Mill Road to Akers Drive (look for the large waterwheel). Follow Akers Drive to Akers Ridge Drive, then turn left and follow Akers Ridge Drive to the parking area on the right.
>
> The Bob Callan trailhead is directly off Interstate North Parkway north of I-285.

The Rottenwood Creek/Bob Callan Trail

The Rottenwood Creek/Bob Callan Trail is very popular with walkers, joggers and bicyclers. On the south end it starts at CRNRA's Paces Mill trailhead

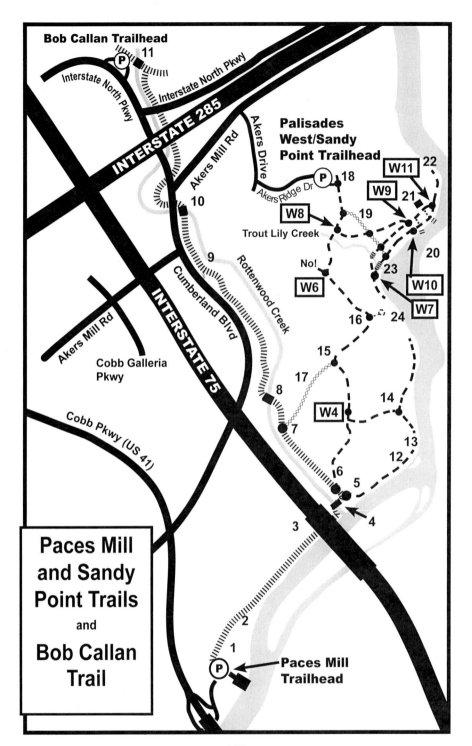

Bob Callan Trailhead

Interstate North Pkwy
Interstate North Pkwy

INTERSTATE 285

Akers Mill Rd
Akers Drive

Palisades
West/Sandy
Point Trailhead

Akers Ridge Dr

W11

W9

W8

W6

Trout Lily Creek

No!

Rottenwood Creek

Cumberland Blvd

INTERSTATE 75

Akers Mill Rd

Cobb Galleria
Pkwy

Cobb Pkwy (US 41)

W4

W10

W7

Paces Mill
and Sandy
Point Trails

and

Bob Callan
Trail

Paces Mill
Trailhead

just off U.S 41 (Cobb Parkway). There, you'll find plenty of parking as well as picnic areas, a restroom facility, and a canoe/raft launching ramp.

From Paces Mill the trail extends northward under Interstate 75 before crossing Rottenwood Creek. It then turns left and follows the creek upstream, eventually leaving CRNRA as it approaches the Bob Callan trailhead off Interstate North Parkway. The Bob Callan Trail portion, a project of the Cumberland Community Improvement District, is named for a former administrator with the Federal Highway Administration. In fact, work is currently underway to extend the Bob Callan Trail all the way to CRNRA's Cochran Shoals Unit.

Start your hike at the parking area off U.S. 41/Cobb Pkwy. From the parking area, the trail skirts a **field (1).** Then, beyond a **concrete manhole (2),** it crosses a creek and enters woods, following the river upstream. Several vantage points offer great views of the water. Spur trails lead toward apartments up on the ridges, but the main trail stays close to the river and soon passes beneath the **Interstate 75 bridge (3).**

A hiker crosses one of the footbridges over Rottenwood Creek.

Beyond the overpass, the trail swings left and then right to cross a **steel bridge over Rottenwood Creek (4)**. Across the bridge, the paved trail turns left to follow the creek upstream. Note the **intersections (5, 6 and 7)** with trails which form part of the central loop hike covered later in this section.

The paved trail eventually crosses the creek again on **another bridge (8).** Beyond that point, it swings away from the creek, leaving the woods as it begins a long climb. That climb continues for not quite a half mile. In years past, a primitive dirt trail remained close to the creek through this section and led to the ruins of a grist mill operated in the 19th century by the Akers brothers. The mill ran on water power but had a back-up engine for use when the creek ran low. The ruins are not accessible from the current paved trail.

Near the top of the hill, near Akers Mill Road, a **short connecting spur (9)** links the main paved trail to Cumberland Blvd. That little connector provides an alternate access point to the paved trail, but it does *not* offer any parking.

Beyond the spur is **yet another bridge (10)** over Rottenwood Creek. This one offers a particularly dramatic view of the rocky streambed below.

The trail soon passes under Cumberland Blvd. (twice) and then under I-285 and Interstate North Parkway. Just beyond Interstate North Parkway is a cross trail, also paved. Turning right puts you on a short spur that leads toward a nearby office building. But turning left quickly takes you to **one more bridge over Rottenwood Creek (11)** – and, beyond that, to the Bob Callan Trail trailhead parking area off Interstate North Parkway.

Central Loop

This guide describes a counterclockwise hike around the central loop, starting at **intersection 5** near the end of the **bridge (4)** over Rottenwood Creek. Look for a dirt trail entering the woods to the right of an info board. Follow that trail upriver. You'll get some great views of the Chattahoochee as you go. But you'll also note (and may even get wind of) candycane-shaped metal vent pipes, reminders of the buried sewer line that also follows this route upstream.

You'll soon reach the downstream end of a **small island (12)**. The channel between island and mainland is a good place to look for waterfowl.

Beyond the upper end of the island, the trail trends left as it approaches a **rocky area (13)** with a small sandy beach nearby. Cross the rocks carefully and continue upstream. Eventually the floodplain widens and the trail swings away from the river, bringing you to an **intersection (14)**. Turning right takes you back toward the river and upstream but soon ends at a massive **rock outcrop (24)** where you have no choice but to turn around and backtrack.

To continue the loop, turn left instead. The trail will climb (sometimes steeply) for about 400 paces and eventually bring you to **intersection W4.**

To complete the loop, go left at W4 for the descent back towards Rottenwood Creek. Steep at first, the descent levels out as you approach the paved path at **intersection 6.** Turn left there to return to **point 5** where you began this loop.

Right at W4: The Sandy Point Connector

Turning right instead of left at intersection W4 puts you on the trail to Sandy Point. More specifically, it launches you on a seemingly endless climb that'll have most hikers feeling their leg muscles (and some hikers gasping for air) by the time it connects with the Sandy Point access trail at **intersection W8.**

Between W4 and W8 are several other intersections. At the first one, **intersection 15,** turn right to stay on the Sandy Point connector. You'll begin to follow a ridge, gently climbing and descending in places but never too steeply. It's very pleasant hiking, especially after that last climb!

Several hundred yards beyond intersection 15, look for a **spur trail (16)** going right. It continues to a loop on the end of a ridge – a sort of hiker's scenic overlook. The views from that end-of-trail loop can be spectacular.

After appreciating the views, return to the main trail and continue toward Sandy Point. You'll soon begin a long descent to **intersection W6,** where you should turn right to stay on the trail and on National Park Service land.

Beyond W6 the trail is relatively level for a while. It then begins to descend toward Trout Lily Creek. After crossing the creek, 150 yards of hiking and several switchbacks will bring you to a deadend at a cross trail at **intersection W8.** To the left is the Sandy Point/Palisades West parking area off Akers Ridge Drive; to the right is the Sandy Point trail network.

But before we move on...what if you had turned *left* at intersection 15? That would put you on a path that comes in like a lamb but ends like that lion. It starts out easy but gets rougher and finally becomes downright terrible as it approaches its junction with the paved Rottenwood Creek Trail. It's no surprise that some hikers call it the **Tribulation Trail (17)**. Despite these rigors, it appears to be heavily used. But I don't recommend it. There's better hiking elsewhere.

Sandy Point trails (from the Akers Ridge Drive parking area)

Everybody loves the trails of Sandy Point, which offer everything from woods to rock cliffs to floodplain wetlands to sparkling river shoals. Hikers delight in this beautiful area. So do some determined kayakers, who come here to hone their whitewater skills in the nearby shoals – and who cheerfully carry kayaks up and down the access trail to do so!

The area is most easily accessed from the parking area off Akers Ridge Drive, where you'll pick up the trail behind the info board. A short connector leads to the **main trail (18)**, where you turn right and begin a long descent along a wide woods road. You'll spot a **spur (19)** going left and downhill, but stay on the main trail.

You'll soon reach **NPS in-**

Left: A family enjoys an afternoon of hiking on the Sandy Point trails. Above: A kayaker carries his boat up the trail from the river at Sandy Point to the Akers Ridge Drive parking area.

Beach areas, river shoals and spectacular rock outcrops are among the many attractions of Sandy Point, making it a favorite among hikers.

tersection **W8.** A right turn there puts you on the connector which carries you to the Central Loop. To reach the Sandy Point area, however, continue downhill on the main trail toward **intersection W9.**

From W9 you can explore a long loop that stretches along the floodplain. Several cut-across trails make this easy to do. Note the small launching ramp near **NPS point W10;** also look across the river to see a **spectacular rock cliff (20).** Upstream from this point is a set of stone steps at river's edge, and a cut-across trail takes you to across the loop to a **restroom building (21).**

Further upstream is **intersection W11.** The trail continues beyond it for a short distance but soon **ends (22)** at a rocky area. Along the way are great views of Devil's Race Course Shoals, where you'll often see kayakers and canoeists testing their skills.

What about the downriver part of the loop? The riverside portion follows the water's edge for a while, then swings away into the woods. Soon, a **bridge and boardwalk (23)** carry you over Trout Lily Creek. Beyond the boardwalk is **NPS intersection W7.** Turning left there takes you back toward the river and downstream; the trail continues until it **ends at a massive rock outcrop (24).** That's the other side of the trail-blocking rock outcrop you encounter when hiking upriver from the Paces Mill parking area, but there's no way around it so you'll have to backtrack.

After exploring the area, return to **intersection W9** and, from there, to the Akers Ridge Drive parking area.

The view of the river from upstream of the Whitewater trailhead

East Palisades

CRNRA's East Palisades unit, often known simply as "Whitewater," offers everything from wetlands and woodlands to rock cliffs and overlooks – and even a forest of bamboo.

There are two primary ways to access the unit's trails. One is via Indian Trail, a gated road leading to a CRNRA parking area. Note that the Indian Trail gate is occasionally closed, and there's no hiker parking *outside* the gate on Indian Trail.

The second major access, easy to reach from I-75 or I-285, is via the parking area off Whitewater Creek Road at the southern end of the unit.

It's also possible to access these trails from the north (at **E18**) via a trailhead (but no parking) off Riverview Road.

This chapter describes several East Palisades hikes, starting with a long loop hike. We'll also look at "the network," a group of trails in the west-central portion of the unit, as well as at the unit's relatively remote north-end trails.

From grand river views to wetlands and rock cliffs (and even a bamboo forest), you'll find it along the many and varied trails of East Palisades

Finding the trailheads

Indian Trail trailhead: From I-285, take exit 22 and pick up Northside Drive going south. Continue south to Indian Trail and turn right. Follow Indian Trail through the gate. The road will become gravel. Continue to the parking area.

Whitewater trailhead: The "Whitewater" trailhead is located off Whitewater Creek Rd. From I-285 exit onto US-41 and go south about 2.2 miles to Mt. Paran Rd. You'll see a large church on your right. Turn left on Mt. Paran Rd. Go about 0.6 miles to Harris Trail and turn left. Continue on Harris Trail to Whitewater Creek Rd. and turn left. The Whitewater entrance is on the right after about a tenth of a mile.

The main loop

The premiere hike at East Palisades is a long loop starting at **point E1.** Hiked clockwise, as here, it takes you along the river, up a ridge, and then along and

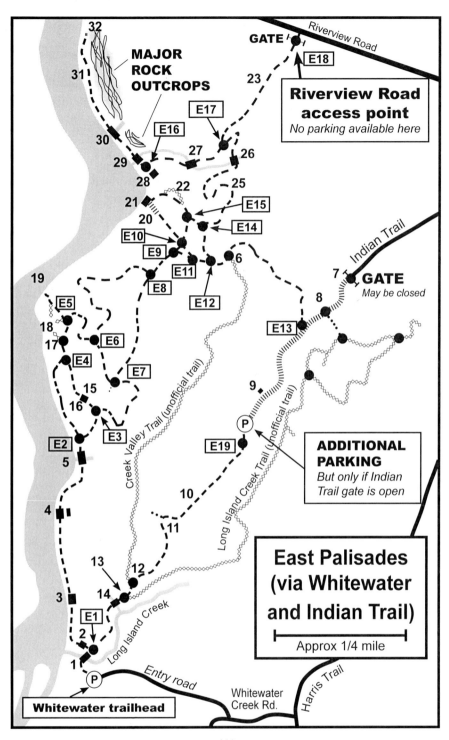

MAJOR ROCK OUTCROPS

GATE

Riverview Road

E18

Riverview Road access point
No parking available here

E17

E16

Indian Trail

E15

E14

E10

E9

E11

E8

E12

GATE
May be closed

E13

E5

E6

E4

E7

E19

P

ADDITIONAL PARKING
But only if Indian Trail gate is open

E2

E3

Creek Valley Trail (unofficial trail)

Long Island Creek Trail (unofficial trail)

East Palisades (via Whitewater and Indian Trail)

Approx 1/4 mile

E1

Long Island Creek

P

Entry road

Whitewater Creek Rd.

Harris Trail

Whitewater trailhead

down the ridge and back to your starting point. This loop can also begin at the Indian Trail parking area.

From the main Whitewater parking area, you'll first notice a well-worn path leading to a sandy beach-like area on the river. But look to the right for the main trailhead at **intersection E1.** Located just across the **footbridge over Long Island Creek (1)**, it's the gateway to the trails of East Palisades.

A portion of the East Palisades main loop hike follows graveled Indian Trail. The gate to the road may be open, so watch for cars on this section of the loop.

From E1, turn left. You'll cross a **small footbridge (2)** over a small branch, then turn right as the trail swings upstream and eventually crosses **another tiny footbridge (3)**. Soon you'll traverse a short **boardwalk (4)** through a wet area. There's a bench at the boardwalk in case you need to take a break to tighten up the ol' hiking shoes, but high water seems to take a regular toll on this bench.

Beyond the bench is the **bridge over Charlie's Trapping Creek (5)** followed by a fork in the trail at **point E2.** To the left is "The Network," a group of trails that crisscross the terrain between the loop trail and the river. But to continue the loop hike, go right.

About 100 paces of level hiking carries you across the floodplain to **point E3.** This section may be very soggy after rain.

At **E3** the trail forks again. Go right to stay on the loop, climbing steeply to **point E7** where you can go straight or turn right. Going straight puts you on another of the network trails, while turning right continues the loop on a trail that carries you uphill and then follows a ridge north. This beautifully forested pathway climbs gently for the next quarter mile or so, bringing you eventually to **point E8.** Turning left there takes you downhill on the northernmost part of the network. But going straight ahead continues the loop.

About 130 paces beyond E8 is **point E9.** To stay on the loop, turn right at E9 and hike downhill. Then, at **intersection E11,** continue straight ahead to **point E12;** to stay on the loop, continue straight at E12 as well.

About 80 paces beyond E12 is an **intersection (6)** with one of two major "unofficial" trails in this unit. A right turn puts you on that trail, which some call the Creek Valley Trail. But go straight to stay on the main trail and continue the loop. It trends generally southeast, treating you to about a third of a mile of relatively easy hiking interrupted occasionally by steeper sections. The trail eventually reaches **point E13** just before Indian Trail Road. To the left, the graveled road extends to a **gate (7)** at the park boundary. When open, that gate provides access to the Indian Trail parking area. However, the gate may be closed. If it's closed, don't park on Indian Trail.

Between E13 and the gate there's a wide, smooth gravel road almost all the way to the gate (only the last few yards before the gate are paved). When hiking that road, remember that it's designed for vehicular traffic. If the Indian Trail gate is open, you're likely to encounter cars there at any time. Be careful.

As you near the gate, look for an **intersection (8)** with a trail that swings off to the right. That's a connector to the north end of what some call the Long Island Creek trail, the second major unofficial trail in East Palisades. But to continue the loop, go right at E13 and follow the road toward the parking area. Along the way, note the great **sitting rock (9)** to the right of the trail.

The trail swings left before arriving at the parking area, then re-enters the woods on its far side behind a cluster of signs. Not far beyond the signs, a map post marking **NPS point E19** will confirm that you're on the right track.

Beyond E19 you'll enjoy easy hiking along the ridge for a bit over 200 yards. Look for the **remains of an old house site (10)** to the right of the trail. Beyond that point, the trail traverses a **switchback (11)** and then begins a long descent that goes on for several hundred yards as the trail drops off the ridge.

Back on the floodplain, look for an **intersection (12)** with a trail that turns right. That's the other end of the unofficial Creek Valley Trail which you encountered earlier at point 9. Not far beyond it is **another intersection (13)**, this one with a well-used trail that swings back and to the left. That's the southern end of the Long Island Creek Trail, the other heavily used but unofficial trail.

To complete the loop, stay on the main trail. You'll almost immediately cross a **footbridge (14)**; to the right is a wetland area that can offer great wildlife watching. Once across the bridge, the trail follows Long Island Creek downstream back to **point E1** and the completion of the loop.

Exploring "the network"

After hiking the loop trail, you'll want to check out "the network," a group of trails that extends to the west of the loop toward the river. These trails can be accessed at E2, E3, E7, and E8). What awaits you along these trails? Here's a look:

E2 to E4: From E2 to E4, you'll follow the edge of the river. This section of trail is essentially level and is easy to follow.

E3 to E4: The E3/E4 segment roughly parallels the E2/E4 segment. It too follows the edge of the floodplain but on the "ridge" side instead of on the "river" side. **Rock outcrops (15)** rise to the right of the trail, especially near the boardwalk which carries the trail over a wet area. Such rocky overhangs were used as shelters by the area's early inhabitants. Also notice the **wet area (16)** on the river side of the boardwalk. It can be good wildlife watching territory.

E4 to E5: This short section ranges from level to *steep!* From E4 to **point 17**, it's a level floodplain trail. The short spur trail heading left from point 17 continues for a just few yards before ending at a **rock outcrop (18)**.

From point 17 the trail climbs steeply to **intersection E5**. There, to your left, a narrow spur extends out onto the same **rock outcrop (18)** that blocked the spur from point 17. This spur passes very close to a steep drop. Use caution.

Two other trails extend from E5. One goes left and downhill, skirting the rock

What about those "unofficial" trails?

One reality of large areas such CRNRA units is that there will be "unofficial" trails. Some are like spring flowers, blossoming and then disappearing almost overnight. But others endure and morph into major footpaths in their own right, sometimes receiving every bit as much use as their more "official" cousins.

East Palisades has two major and well used "unofficial" trails." You may find yourself on one or the other of them at some point. Thus, in the interest of completeness, they are shown on the unit map and are briefly described here.

The Creek Valley Trail

First up is a trail that many hikers call the Creek Valley Trail. Accessible from the main loop trail at points 6 and 12, this trail runs up a little valley that roughly parallels the river. The southern portion of this trail more or less follows a small creek upstream, and the bottomland can be prime wildlife watching territory. It's a favorite haunt of some serious birders.

As this trail works its way up the valley, it skirts wetlands and passes rocky cliffs. Along the way the trail fords the creek several times.

At its northern end, as it climbs out of the valley and up the ridge on its way back to the main loop at point 6, this trail becomes very steep and challenges you with some rugged hiking.

The Long Island Creek Trail

The Long Island Creek Trail, a second major unofficial trail at Palisades East, begins near the south end of the main loop at point 13. It initially follows Long Island Creek upstream before moving away from the creek to traverse a roller-coaster ridge flank as it heads toward its eventual intersection with the graveled portion of Indian Trail at point 8. The ridge flank portion of the trail is characterized by numerous gully crossings, some of which offer potentially tricky footing.

At its north end of this trail is a winding loop which skirts close to the edge of NPS property in several places. There are many spurs leading from the main trail, and these can be confusing.

It is not at all uncommon to meet cross-country joggers on this trail. A number of birders say that they enjoy this trail as well.

outcrop and leading to a great view of **Thornton Shoals (19)**. Along the way another spur makes a sharp left and goes back toward the rock outcrop; it ends at a near-vertical rock face.

E5 to E6: From E5 toward E6, the trail begins to climb, passing the huge root ball of a massive fallen tree. The trail then dips to cross a tiny creek before resuming its climb toward **E6,** which awaits you just past a little switchback.

E6 to E7: The trail from E6 to E7 is initially very steep with *lots* of roots in the trail – but only for short distance. Once beyond them, the trail moderates as it approaches E7, the intersection with the main loop trail described earlier.

E6 to E8: This section of trail is a long, steady climb. Many consider this one of the most scenic sections of trail in East Palisades, and it's easy to see why. Depending on leaf cover, the views of the Chattahoochee can be incredible.

Overlook platform

If you like overlooks, don't miss the platform west of E10/E15. From E10, follow a gradually descending trail for about 110 paces to a **long set of 52 timber steps (20)** leading down a fairly steep incline to the **observation platform (21)** itself. It's a leg-stretcher, but you'll be rewarded by great vistas of the river and of part of the suburban Atlanta skyline.

An alternate approach is via E15. This approach offers an easier grade with no steps. Just beyond E15 a **side trail (22)** forks right and parallels the main trail

The East Palisades observation platform provides spectacular views of the river and of the suburban Atlanta skyline.

for a short distance, but on the "platform" end of that side trail the last few yards are rough and steep. Stay on the main trail for the easiest hiking.

The north-end trails

You haven't fully experienced East Palisades until you've explored this unit's north-end trails. Accessed via intersection E14 (or from the Riverview Road trailhead) they are just the thing for hikers who want a total hiking experience.

Most hikers access the north end trails from the loop hike via **intersection E14**. From E14 to **intersection E17** the trail drops (sometimes steeply) through a **series of switchbacks and sharp descents (25)**, fording a couple of wet-weather branches before arriving at a **wooden footbridge (26)** over a creek. A spur turns upstream at the bridge, but stay on the main trail.

Across the bridge, the trail turns right and goes upstream for several dozen yards before turning sharply left. Not far beyond that point, you'll ford a small branch, then climb up to a sharp switchback to your left to **E17**. A right turn at that intersection puts you on a long climb to the Riverview Road trailhead. But stay on the main trail, heading downhill to a **footbridge (27)** over a creek. Across the bridge, continue down the creek to **intersection E16** and the river.

This small wood footbridge carries hikers over a small creek near the north end of East Palisades.

To the left of E16 is the **stone foundation of an old cabin (28).** To the right the trail continues upriver, crossing a **stone bridge (29)** over the same creek you crossed earlier. Beyond the bridge look for large rock outcrops to the right of the trail. Eventually the rock gives way to a creek, crossed via a **footbridge (30).** The rock reappears beyond the footbridge, becoming more and more dramatic as you go. It will be your constant companion for the duration of your hike.

But then the rock is forgotten as something new comes into view – a stand of bamboo. At first it's just a few tall stalks among the trees, but then suddenly you're in the midst of an honest-to-goodness **bamboo forest (31)**. Thousands of stalks stretch skyward all around you, some measuring several inches in diameter and goodness knows how many feet tall. A spiderweb of side trails leads into this patch of giant grass, inviting you to explore. You'll probably spend more time than you'd intended wandering through this unexpected delight.

So what can you do in a bamboo forest? Aside from getting a sore neck looking upward at soaring stalks, I found that I could walk from stalk to stalk and tap the segments to generate a range of vaguely musical tones. Sometimes I'd get a high pitch; sometimes it was lower. Given enough time, I'm sure I could have come up with a symphony of music notes there among the giant tubular grass.

The bamboo patch extends for perhaps 200 yards, and beyond its end it's not far to the end of this trail. Those riverside rock outcrops are creeping closer to the river, and the trail – having no choice – finally fades as it attempts to climb them. It's possible to work your way up the **rocks (32)** for some commanding views of the river, but it is a workout to get there. It can be a tough climb.

It was especially tough on one hike last summer. The temperature was in the high 90s, and I'd taken water. But the heat pulled it out as fast as I poured it in. Still, I had to make it to the end to put the period on the sentence, as they say. If you're a hiker, you'll understand.

And so I was sweating my way up to my favorite observation point when I saw it: an unopened bottle of water tucked away underneath a little shelf of rock in one of the few shady spots to be found. There was a note tucked away with the can. It read, "You made it, so this one's for you."

You've got to love hiking in the urban backcountry!

A forest of bamboo is one of the surprises waiting for you when you hike to the north end of East Palisades.

Volunteer at CRNRA!

The Chattahoochee River National Recreation Area has one of the most dedicated full-time staffs that you'll find. But like many parks, it also relies on the contributions of volunteers – including volunteers like you!

Many CRNRA volunteers give of their time on a regular basis, becoming involved in long-term projects or ongoing programs. But even if you don't have a lot of time to spare, you may be able to contribute a few hours now and then – perhaps during a special event or scheduled work day.

A variety of volunteer opportunities are available. Here's a sampling:

Trail Building and Maintenance – It takes a good bit of effort to maintain more than 50 miles of hiking trails in the many units of CRNRA, and there are plenty of opportunities to help with trail maintenance and development.

Have you enjoyed the many fine hiking opportunities offered by the Chattahoochee River National Recreation Area? You can "pay it forward" and ensure more great outdoor experiences for others in the future by becoming a CRNRA volunteer!

Non-Native Species Control – Work with individuals and groups to remove non-native, invasive plants and make a visible difference in the park.

Trash clean-up – Help clear out trash from the river!

Special Events – Greet visitors, staff booths, haul boats and handle other tasks during special events at the park.

Programs – Volunteers can help students learn about the rich natural and cultural heritage of the park.

Trail Blazers – Provide an additional set of eyes and ears for park staff along the 48-mile stretch of the river.

You may have other skills that could benefit the park, too. Don't hesitate to offer to put them to work in the ongoing program at CRNRA.

"If you have a skill, then we can use it," says Scott Pfeninger, chief of park operations.

To learn how you can volunteer at the Chattahoochee River National Recreation Area, go to **http://www.nps.gov/chat/supportyourpark/volunteer.htm** or contact the park at (678) 538-1200.

TRAIL NOTES

TRAIL NOTES